CW00867918

A Spring Ramble

Walking the Offa's Dyke Path

John Davison

A Spring Ramble – Walking the Offa's Dyke Path

First edition, 2015.

© John Davison, 2015.

The right of John Davison to be identified as the author of this work has been asserted by him in accordance with the Copyright, Designs and Patents Act, 1988.

All rights reserved. No part of this publication may be reproduced, stored in a retrieval system, or transmitted, in any form or by any means without the prior written permission of the publisher, nor be otherwise circulated in any form of binding or cover other than that in which it is published and without a similar condition being imposed on the subsequent purchaser.

Cover photograph: Eglwyseg, © John Davison, 2015.

To Mum

About the Author

John Davison started hiking and camping on school trips and in the Scouts, during the early 1970s. Exploring new places, meeting new people and discovering how the two interrelate is an interest which has never left him.

John is a Fellow of the Royal Geographical Society and he lives in Essex, UK.

Contents

Part 1

Walking the Walk

Chapter 1

The Wye Valley

My journal for this walk starts with some plain speaking. "Train to Chepstow", it says, as if that's all that needs to be said.

Three words to sum up the journey to the start of my walk. Three words that give no indication of the gradual release of cares as my train pushed further down the line from London into the West Country in springtime. General, workaday cares and worries that gradually disappeared like morning dew as it dries in the sunshine, to be replaced by a new and different list, specific to the task ahead of me.

The dew-and-sunshine metaphor was an apt one while the sun was shining, but the day felt as if it couldn't make up its mind what season it wanted to be a part of. Blue sky and sunshine gave the impression that winter was over at last, but every couple of hours, dark clouds blew in and spoiled it all.

I changed trains at Newport, and while I was waiting on the "up" platform I noticed two ladies-of-a-certain-age. They stood out because they were dressed for walking in a way that only the British seem to do. Sensible sweaters, rugged multi-pocketed trousers, heavy canvas rucksacks and big clumpy boots, all combined with cut-glass English accents to separate them from the Welsh commuters who surrounded them.

The Offa's Dyke Path is a national trail and we were near to the start of it, so I expected to encounter other walkers. However, since many people dress like that simply to walk the dog, it was impossible to guess whether they were about to embark on the same trail as I was, or if they were just out for an afternoon stroll. I sneaked a look at the map strapped to one of their packs, but it didn't help. I decided that if I had to commit myself, I'd make an educated guess that we were going to do the same walk.

My impression was confirmed when we boarded the same train and all alighted together at Chepstow station.

The Offa's Dyke Path doesn't start at Chepstow, but Chepstow is the nearest transport hub and it's as near as dammit to Sedbury Cliffs, which is where I needed to be.

But first things first, and I headed into town to get some lunch, while the ladies struck out in a different direction.

It's impossible to pass through Chepstow and not notice the River Wye. The river is broad and muddy as it passes through the town, very near to its junction with the Severn, and here the Wye has one of the highest tidal ranges in the world, second only to the Bay of Fundy in Canada.

In this area, the River Wye was established as the border between England and Wales by the first King of England, Athelstan, in 928CE[1]. A century or so later, Chepstow

---

[1] *See the Timeline in Appendix A (p119) for help with dates.*

became important to the Normans because it controlled the Wye, and thus river access to the town of Hereford and the area of the Marches. It was also the lowest bridging site on the river and so an important access point into Wales.

The importance of the town to the Normans is evidenced by the date of the castle: it was commenced in 1067, just a year after the Conquest. To warrant such rapid and expensive fortification Chepstow must have been significant, but with the end of the wars between England and Wales in the 1400s, the castle's importance declined. That said, it's still the oldest surviving stone castle in Britain, and it still looms large and powerful over the town, as a castle should.

Although my map showed very little forest on the edges of Chepstow, the town seemed wrapped and enfolded by green trees, almost embraced by them. The trees and the castle, with the river, created an illusion that felt almost timeless. I say "illusion" because the town has experienced a lot of change and continues to do so.

Replete after lunch in a chip shop, I checked my map and set out for Sedbury Cliffs, the official start of my trek.

I walked down the main street, past the occasional boarded up shop, pondering as I did so on the difficult commercial struggle that small towns face if they are to remain reasonable places in which to live. It seems that we want the shops and we expect them to continue trading, but we don't want to shop in them because we can buy cheaper in out-of-town retail parks or online, and most of us fail to appreciate the contradiction.

I paused on the road bridge over the River Wye and looked out across the old wharves and industrial areas by the river. The port of Chepstow thrived in medieval times because it was controlled by a Marcher Lord and so was exempt from

English taxation. For many years it was the biggest port in Wales. Now, port activity and shipbuilding are a rarity.

But impressions are ethereal, intangible things, and sometimes it's difficult to say with any certainty why we feel as we do. Despite the occasional boarded up shop and the industrial sites waiting to be transformed into housing, I got the impression that Chepstow was trying hard and I liked the place.

I turned and carried on across the bridge. Athelstan's 928 border is still in place here, and so as I crossed the Wye I was passing back into England. A large, battered sign welcomed me to England in two languages, English and Welsh.

I wondered who pays for all that dual-language stuff.

All public bodies in Wales are required by law to treat the English and Welsh languages equally, a fact which must be largely responsible for any demand there is for Welsh language graduates, since without those laws their career prospects would be slight. But it can't be cheap to double your production of letters, forms and signage so that they all include two languages.

Is such expenditure a prudent use of public finances? An assessment based purely on the numbers might indicate that it's not: the last census showed that only 19% of people in Wales could speak Welsh, and that was down 2% from the time of the preceding census. I was walking out of Chepstow, a town in which just 9% of residents regard themselves as Welsh speakers.

Can a price be put on a language? How do you express your culture and your history if you allow your language to die and you have to use someone else's? The public purse isn't bottomless though, so presumably someone, somewhere, must have decided that the subsidies and the promotions are a reasonable use of public money. But that begs the question, should a language be pushed and promoted at all? Isn't there a case for saying that people will speak it if they want to, and that if they don't, it will fall by the wayside? If a language can't survive in its own right without, so to speak, having air blown into its lungs at regular intervals, is it really a living language?

And how do you keep your enthusiasm to preserve your language in proportion? I recalled a spirited correspondence I'd had a few years ago with officers of Her Majesty's Revenue and Customs, in which I tried valiantly to convince them they were wasting time and money by sending documents written in Welsh to me in east London. (They said they were required to by law because the tax office was based in Wales. Eventually sanity prevailed, and they apologised and stopped doing it).

But the central question remains: who pays for all this hoo-hah? As an Englishman, I have no interest in whether the Welsh language thrives or whether it dies. I don't wish it ill, but neither do I wish to contribute towards the cost of keeping it alive. But nowhere can I find out who is paying.

I just hope it isn't me.

The sun was out and I was striding across a meadow towards Sedbury Cliffs when I was shaken from my reverie by two figures approaching me from the other side of the field. As they got closer, I saw they were the two ladies I'd travelled with on the train earlier.

They stopped and I managed to get from them that, yes, like me, they were walking the Offa's Dyke Path. Beyond that they were uncommunicative and plainly they did not wish to linger in my company.

That took me back a little bit. For me, part of the joy of walking is the people I meet along the way. That goes double for a named and signed trail because a well-known path attracts walkers and on the most famous trails you have the pleasure of chatting with people from all over the world. I hadn't envisaged a lot of back-slapping and hail-fellow-well-met sort of stuff, but I had looked forward to a bit of a chat about our common interest. That wasn't to be, and they were quickly on their way, leaving me to wander the last, pensive mile to Sedbury Cliffs.

I was the only person on the cliffs and I quickly found the large stone marking the start of my walk. The plaque on the stone (yes, in English and Welsh, in case you're asking) told me I had 168 miles to go to reach my destination, the seafront in the north-Walian town of Prestatyn. This was nine miles shorter than my researches had indicated, but most authorities now quote 177 miles for this walk, so I knew I wouldn't get away with 168.

I paused and looked around me. I couldn't help feeling that such a momentous moment deserved more. The grass was a bright, almost luminous green; the sky was blue with high, white clouds scudding across it. The Bristol Channel glistened like liquid mud and the sun shone down, highlighting the big suspension bridge spanning the Severn estuary.

I sat on the stone and took a swig of water from my water bottle.

When, I wondered, did our society lose its reverence for technology? I remembered walking across that bridge in 1969 with my parents and it was an awe-inspiring experience. The bridge was quite new then, and I remember the motorway service area constructed nearby. The "services" were built with a viewing area in the restaurant, so that diners could sit there, and eat and drink, while looking out at the bridge. There was even a viewing area outside where you could sit and picnic, and look at the bridge. People didn't just stop there for a break on long motorway journeys: many of them went to those services specifically to see the bridge.

I couldn't think of a modern-day equivalent, a structure wholly functional but which is so admired that families take a day out purely to look at it. A more recent feat of engineering, the Queen Elizabeth II Bridge over the River Thames at Dartford, was deliberately designed so that it cannot be used by pedestrians. The QE2 Bridge (as it's known for short) used to have a viewing area nearby, but it's long been locked, vandalised and strewn with fly-tipped rubbish. The idea of anyone going there if they didn't have to is ridiculous, the thought of families going there for a day out is surreal.

Then again, Technology made some pretty big promises in the 1960s. In a few years, we expected to be riding around on jet-packs and living on the moon, so maybe we got disillusioned when it turned out that Technology didn't have all the answers.

I sighed and tucked my water bottle away. Enough of this. It was time to start.

I stood up and shouldered my pack. The dyke stretched away in front of me, running downhill along the left edge of a field, with a wood on its left. The trees did not extend onto the dyke, but their higher branches arched over it, providing dappled patches of shade on the short, green grass. A small stream ran down the field and cut through the low dyke at right angles, to enter the wood beyond.

17

The Offa's Dyke Path is a national trail that follows the England-Wales border for most of its length. 285km long (that's 177 miles in old money), it was opened in 1971 by Lord Hunt, the leader of the first successful attempt on Everest, in 1953. About a third of the path follows the eighth century earthwork known as Offa's Dyke.

Offa was King of Mercia from 757 to 796CE. Mercia equates roughly to the English Midlands of today, but the area under Offa's control stretched wider than that, making him probably the most powerful monarch in England in his time.

The dyke which bears his name separated the western edge of Offa's realm from the areas controlled by the princes of Wales. The earthwork consisted of a ditch and a bank, with the ditch on the Welsh side, and there may have been a fence or a paling on the top of the dyke. The dyke was 8m high (from the ditch bottom) and together with the ditch, about 27m wide. Offa's Dyke is often described as the most impressive monument of its kind anywhere in Europe.

Although the dyke seems to have been quickly abandoned, its influence on behaviour and mindset continued for centuries in this turbulent region. Victorian traveller George Borrow noted in his book, *Wild Wales*, that in olden times, "It was customary for the English to cut off the ears of every Welshman found east of the dyke, and for the Welsh to hang every Englishman whom they found to the west of it."

While Borrow's assertion might have been anecdotal, bear it in mind: it sets the scene for much of the history to be found along this walk. History which is belied by the present-day tranquillity of the area, but history nonetheless.

The Offa's Dyke Path can be walked north to south or, as I

intended, south to north, so my journey would begin by the sea at Sedbury Cliffs in England and end by the sea in Prestatyn, in north Wales.

In the process I would walk the length of Wales. I would ascend (and descend) 9,085m. In imperial measurement that's about 29,000 feet, over a thousand feet more than if I started at sea level and climbed Mount Everest, Lord Hunt's old stamping ground.

The highest point on my route would be a mere 703m, just before Hay Bluff, and that fact, combined with the knowledge that I'd make over 9,000m of ascent throughout the whole walk, suggested to me that very little of it would be flat. The highest point on the walk isn't very high, I reasoned, and I knew I'd be starting and finishing at sea level. From that I deduced that I was going to be walking uphill and downhill an awful lot on the Offa's Dyke Path if I was going to total 9,085m of ascent.

I strode downhill along the top off the dyke, over the little footbridge that crosses the stream, and back towards the houses of Pennsylvania, on the edge of Sedbury.

At first glance, the houses here look like typical post-World War 1 social housing of the "homes fit for heroes" era. In fact, they're older than that and they were built for people who came from hundreds of miles away.

Three of these garden suburbs were built, two in Chepstow and one here at Pennsylvania. They were designed to house the 6,000 skilled shipyard workers and their families who were brought south from the shipyards on the Clyde and the Tyne to help the war effort.

The plan was an imperfect solution to a desperate problem.

In 1916, the British were losing over 300,000 tons of shipping to German U-boats *each month.* The country was nowhere near self-sufficient in terms of raw materials and food, and anti-submarine warfare was in its infancy and doing little to mitigate the German attacks.

The government proposed to resolve the problem by the only means anyone could think of: building merchant ships at a great rate. The UK's supply routes were to be kept open not by sinking enemy submarines, but by building merchant ships faster than the Germans could sink them. The ships and their crews would become the targets in a vast shooting gallery, where the lucky would make it across the ocean and the unlucky would go to the bottom.

Three government-owned "National Shipyards" were proposed, one at Chepstow and others at nearby Beachley and Portbury. The ships were to be built quickly, to a prefabricated pattern, and would be assembled in the three new yards. The houses for the workers were built by the Royal Engineers and German prisoners of war.

Despite all the work, very little real progress was made and only one ship was launched before the end of hostilities in 1918. The houses endure though, and form a pleasant enough garden suburb.

I wandered on, soon regaining the Wye, this time on the English bank which provided me with spectacular views westwards from the high river cliffs.

I passed Wintour's Leap, the cliff named after the Royalist Sir John Wintour who, it is said, jumped from the clifftop on his horse to escape pursuing Parliamentary soldiers in the English Civil War. Wintour is supposed to have landed in the river and swum downstream to safety at Chepstow Castle.

It's a good story and Wintour did escape from Parliamentarians on two occasions, but neither of them, historians believe, occurred on this spot. The tale must have made for a romantic interlude though, on the fashionable Wye Tour a century later in the 1700s. I peered over the cliff edge at the dull mud and the shiny brown river 90m below me and shuddered. I wouldn't have fancied it.

I re-joined Offa's Dyke a little way after Wintour's Leap, still up high, and I was passing through what the information boards call "ancient broadleaved woodland", with occasional glimpses of the twisted river meanders over the drop to my left. It was far too early to camp, but I could have stopped there just to savour the sheer beauty off the place, to maximise my time there and to absorb what it offered.

I saw very few people along this stretch, away from the town: a young couple unloading rock-climbing gear from their car, and an older couple in robust trousers and no-nonsense boots out for an afternoon stroll.

The Devil's Pulpit didn't detain me for long – it's just a column of rock overlooking the river and the ruins of Tintern Abbey on the other bank. Legend has it that the Devil preached from here, trying to tempt the monks in the abbey below to leave their holy order and follow him. They didn't, of course.

I'm often struck by how frequently English place names include the Devil. Just off the top of my head I can recall the Devil's Copse, the Devil's Punch Bowl, the Devil's Elbow, the Devil's Quoit, the Devil's Beef Tub and the Devil's Dyke. Britain's national mapping agency, the Ordnance Survey, notes that over 80 places "belong to the Devil", but I reckon that's a cautious estimate.

I wonder what the fascination is? Place names featuring the Devil usually relate to distinct landforms. Perhaps they were pre-Christian pagan sites and the early church was trying to encourage people away from them by suggesting a link to the Devil and to Hell. Most of the names are so old it's impossible to tell.

I paused, struck by the superb view of the abbey ruins down below, hazy in the late afternoon sunshine. It was easy to see how the abbey has provided inspiration for poets and artists through the years. Turner found himself stimulated to paint, while Wordsworth and Tennyson were both moved to write, as was Alan Ginsberg after an acid trip at Tintern in more modern times.

Obviously, the abbey hasn't always been a ruin. It was founded in 1131 by the Cistercian order, who operated to the basic Cistercian principles of obedience, poverty, chastity, silence, prayer, and work.

What a beautiful spot for such a grim code of life! But it all came crashing down when King Henry VIII escalated his dispute with the Church of Rome by appropriating all church property and income in his realm. What became known as the Dissolution of the Monasteries, in 1536, pretty much ended monastic life in Britain, and Tintern became a picturesque ruin for the next 500 years.

"'All kings is mostly rapscallions', said Huckleberry Finn." I smiled to myself and started walking again.

On the hillside up above the hamlet of Brockweir, I found a small, flat area just inside the treeline and set up my tent. I like to keep a low profile when I'm camping, so after the tent was up, I took a few paces across the field and looked back into the wood. My tent was hardly visible.

It was a glorious, warm, spring evening, the clear sky suggesting that a cooler night was on the way. I sipped tea and watched the sun set in the west, behind Wales, and wondered what was ahead of me on my walk.

In the early hours, I was half-awoken by rain pattering on the tent. I woke up fully at five o'clock and took a look outside.

Still raining.

One of the delights of walking without a return rail ticket is the freedom that it provides: freedom from the tyranny of the destination. With no set itinerary I didn't have to get up in the rain and walk a target distance. I could afford to roll over and have another hour in bed, and that's exactly what I did.

By the time I'd finished breakfast, the rain had petered out to become just a general feeling of dampness. I packed up under overcast skies and headed down the hill into the village of Brockweir.

Brockweir was quiet at that time of the morning, and the sight of the village pub made me wonder if I shouldn't have pressed on a little further the evening before. I didn't want to retrace my steps unnecessarily, so if I had dropped into the pub for dinner I would have had to walk onwards from the village in order to find a place to camp, and when I'd checked my map the path north of Brockweir hadn't seemed to offer many possible sites. Had I but realised it, being thwarted at hostelries was to become a defining feature of my walk.

There didn't seem to be enough of Brockweir to sustain a pub and I wondered how it stayed in business. Not by offering cooked breakfasts, that much was sure, I thought, as I passed it, dark and quiet. Directly opposite, I turned onto the path by the river.

In the eighteenth and nineteenth centuries the River Wye was much busier than it is today, and most of the people in Brockweir had some connection with the river trade. The village was the last tidal quay for boats travelling up the Wye, and upstream of this point the water was too shallow for larger vessels. Goods were brought downstream on barges to Brockweir's small quay, where they were transferred to larger, seagoing ships for onward transport.

The quay has been nicely restored and is very pleasant spot. In 1967 the remains of a 31 ton steamboat, La Belle Marie, were discovered there.

La Belle Marie had been owned by a local family, the Dibdens. Before the First World War, the Dibdens ran a ferry service across the River Wye at Brockweir. They knew that a bridge was planned, and that it would quickly make their ferry service redundant, so they sought to diversify.

James Dibden bought La Belle Marie as a market boat, to run agricultural produce, fish and livestock downriver to Chepstow. The boat came back upstream with goods for the general store, which was run by another member of the Dibden family, Susannah.

Now, both boat and store are long gone.

The Offa's Dyke Path has a high route and a low route along this section, and by walking through Brockweir, I'd chosen to take the lower path along the River Wye.

There's something about a river that engages my attention; maybe the ceaseless movement of the water, the potential for travel, upstream or down, or the subtle differences in the lifestyles of the locals because they have a river on their doorstep. One is always in the presence of dynamism when close to a river. It would be difficult to be immobile when Nature is so obviously in motion.

My path was mostly flat, winding across grass fields along the small floodplain of the Wye, narrow between its wooded cliffs to left and right. I met one other person: a man out emptying his dog. He bade me a cheery good morning and, when he learned of my intended destination, he wished me luck and strode purposefully on his way. I suspected that someone at home was preparing a cooked breakfast for him and the thought made me feel like an outsider in this narrow little river valley.

A short section of road walking took me to an uphill stretch through a bluebell wood. A bluebell wood always gladdens my spirit and quickens my blood. Bluebells are a firm indication that spring is giving way to summer, and I'd defy anyone not to feel uplifted by that gauzy blue haze stretching away into the quiet woods. Mix it, as here, with white patches of wild garlic and you have an enchanting scene.

I emerged from the wood into a field and checked my map. The village of Lower Redbrook was next, with two pubs, neither of which would be open at this early hour.

The false ceiling of low, white cloud still covered the sky, but the day had begun to warm and I found myself taking off a layer of clothing. Before long I was generating more body heat by striding up the side of a hill called The Kymin.

The Kymin is 257m high and it overlooks the River Wye, an attribute which has made it a popular picnic spot since at least the 1700s. My map showed a "naval temple" there. We were some miles from the sea, and I had no idea what a naval temple might be doing on The Kymin, or even what one was.

I soon found out as I walked through the trees on top of the hill. A small, walled garden surrounded an elaborate, rectangular stone building. Headed, "BRITAIN'S GLORY", the building is a monument to the Royal Navy and its victories at sea in the eighteenth century. Not a memorial, and I think it's important to make that distinction, but a celebration of the routing of the country's enemies. A plaque on the side reads:

> "The figure which crowns the temple exhibits Britannia, seated on a rock: the painting in front, represents the standard of Great-Britain, waving triumphant over the fallen and captive flags of France, Spain, and Holland: the opposite side, the glorious and ever-memorable Battle of the Nile."

The Naval Temple stands just before a roundhouse, and the roundhouse was constructed in 1794 by a local gentlemen's dining club, as a suitable venue for their meetings. This same group of gentleman-diners erected the Naval Temple nearby in 1800 to celebrate the second anniversary of the Battle of the Nile and sixteen British admirals who had won glory in various theatres of war.

This was a stirring age: stunning naval victories in the war against France had resulted in the Royal Navy becoming seen as a key component of Britishness. Britain is often represented by the female figure of Britannia, and by 1797 Britannia's traditional spear had been replaced by a maritime trident to reflect the ascendancy of the Navy. As you might expect, the Britannia at The Kymin proudly holds a trident, not a spear. A few years later, in 1805, success at Trafalgar would win Britain control of the world's seas for well over a century.

I walked down from The Kymin through Scots pines and holly trees, and into Monmouth for lunch.

My first choice was the ancient Kings Head pub, a building awash with history. But they were having their kitchen refurbished and would not, they assured me, be serving food for the foreseeable future. At this stage of my walk, I still hadn't realised the way the stars were aligned when it came to food and drink, pubs and cafés.

Breakfast had been at six in the morning and my stomach was rumbling. I was in no mood to traipse up and down the high street comparing eateries, so I crossed the road to a chip shop, found myself a table and ordered chicken and chips.

I was just in time because no sooner had I started my meal than the chippy's main source of income arrived: schoolkids in their lunch break. Lots of them. I shovelled chips and mushy peas down my neck, trying all the while not to look like a dosser to the bored kids in the queue for the counter. Eventually I finished, just as an elderly German couple arrived. We chatted as I gave up my table for them and they expressed wonderment that anyone who had any choice in the matter would travel the length of Wales using only his feet.

By the time I got back outside, the sky was darkening and rain looked imminent. I took myself over the road to see what there was of Monmouth Castle. Not very much, as it turned out, but what there was, was strangely moving.

As is so often the case with any site of possible strategic worth in Britain, Monmouth Castle was slighted[2] after the Civil War. Despite that, it's one of few British castles which is still occupied by the military and nowadays it is home to

---

[2] *A castle is "slighted" when it is destroyed or partially demolished to negate its military value in any future conflict.*

the Royal Monmouthshire Royal Engineers (Militia). There can't be many regiments with the word "royal" twice in their name, and to add to its distinction, the Royal Monmouthshire Royal Engineers (Militia) is the most senior regiment in the British Army.

But it wasn't any of that which moved me. Monmouth is very proud of the fact that it is the birthplace of King Henry V, who famously beat a much greater French force at the Battle of Agincourt in 1415. There are four young trees growing in a neat line near the castle. They came, according to a nearby plate, from the grave pits at Agincourt.

Monmouth also holds the dubious distinction of being the last place in Britain where a sentence of "hanged, drawn and quartered" was passed by a criminal court.

Used as a punishment and a deterrent for serious offences for many years, this penalty was a grisly one. If you were so sentenced, you could expect to be hanged by the neck until you were almost dead, then taken down and able to watch as you were cut open and your insides removed and burned in front of you. Next, you were butchered into quarters so that your head and limbs could be displayed on city bridges and gates as a warning to others, and all in front of an enthusiastic crowd. Incredibly, the sentence was still on the statute books in 1840, albeit reserved for that most serious of offences: high treason.

Three men who had taken part in a Chartist riot in neighbouring Newport were charged with high treason and tried in Monmouth's Shire Hall. They were all found guilty and sentenced to be hanged, drawn and quartered.

In Britain, very often the only element which differentiates a lunatic idea from accepted normality seems to be time. Commercial radio and all-day pub opening, for instance, seem completely mainstream now, but started out in the election manifesto of the Official Monster Raving Loony Party. So it was with The People's Charter of 1839.

The Chartists campaigned for six major reforms to the British electoral system. Although many people regarded them as dangerous revolutionaries at the time, all but one of the Chartists' aims were implemented and are now long-accepted components of our democracy. They wanted:

1. Universal male suffrage (at that time the right to vote was confined to a small number of people)

2. No property-owning qualification to become a Member of Parliament (the requirement to own property excluded poorer people from standing for election),

3. Annual parliaments,

4. Equal representation (i.e. electoral districts to be of equal size),

5. Payment for MPs (without a salary only the wealthy could afford to stand for Parliament),

6. Voting in elections to be by secret ballot (to prevent intimidation and bribery).

Some were prepared to go further than others to achieve these reforms, hence the riot in Newport in which 22 people (all Chartists) were killed by soldiers.

Fortunately, after a campaign on behalf of the three men convicted at Monmouth, the Prime Minister announced that the sentence would be commuted to one of transportation to Tasmania. Interestingly, one of the Chartists involved in the

Newport riot (but not in the trial) was Allan Pinkerton, later the founder of the famous detective agency.

The River Wye is joined by the River Monnow in Monmouth, and the Monnow Bridge sits at the bottom end of Monnow Street, the town's main shopping thoroughfare. I strolled down the narrow pavements of Monmouth's long high street, carrying my trekking poles and trying not to sideswipe inattentive pedestrians with my rucksack. I could see the bridge at the end of the street, its distinctive gatehouse towering over the narrow carriageway below.

Monnow Bridge was built in the 1200s as a barrier against the Welsh and as a toll collection point, and it's the only intact medieval fortified bridge in Britain. As I walked through its main arch, with a backdrop of leaden skies, the fortified gatehouse felt ominous. But I'd crossed into an area of tree-lined residential streets and my mind was fixed on my journey, so the feeling quickly dissipated. I wanted to reach the White Castle that evening, to give me a good chance of making Hay-on-Wye the day after, so I struck on out of Monmouth.

As I walked, I mused on the enigma that is Monmouthshire.

When I was a boy, Monmouthshire was marked on maps as part of England. Nowadays it's very definitely part of Wales. But it's much more confusing than that.

After the Norman invasion in 1066, the Normans set about assessing exactly what assets they had conquered, by means of the Domesday Survey. The product of that survey, the Domesday Book, shows the area that we now call Monmouthshire as part of England, but it was located in that part of England on the border with Wales which was known as the March and controlled by the Marcher Lords. Marcher Lords were appointed by the king and given complete jurisdiction over their subjects without recourse to the law of England. This meant that "Monmouthshire" was in England but was not subject to English law.

In 1535, King Henry VIII integrated Wales and the March into the English legal system by the Laws in Wales Act. This Act created the county of Monmouthshire and cited it in the list of Welsh counties.

However, another Act of the same name, passed just a few years later in 1542, did *not* include Monmouthshire in the list of Welsh counties. This ambiguity was to continue almost until the present day. For centuries, Acts of Parliament relating only to Wales referred to "Wales and Monmouthshire", and the actual line of the English/Welsh border mattered very little in practice.

That began to change as Welsh identity developed more fully in the nineteenth century and the status of Monmouthshire became a subject of dispute. The problem persisted until the reorganisation of counties effected by the Local Government Act 1972 settled the matter once and for all, and Monmouthshire stayed (or, depending on your point of view, became) Welsh.

As I pressed on, the ceiling of solid white cloud gradually cleared, as if wiped from the sky by a giant hand. A pleasant evening was in the offing.

I passed through cider orchards, the neat lines of apple trees white with blossom, made even brighter by the afternoon sunshine. Unfortunately for me, there was no sign of the product of all that industry, so it was with thirst unslaked that I eventually arrived at the White Castle and started thinking about a spot to camp.

Chapter 2

Across the Black Mountains

The White Castle, in a nice piece of yin and yang, sits on a hillside just before the path rises into the Black Mountains.

Dating from the twelfth century, the White Castle looks as any self-respecting ruined castle should: obviously uninhabitable but still substantial enough to be interesting. Unfortunately for me, it didn't matter how interesting the castle was, I wasn't allowed in. I'd had the temerity to approach it on a Tuesday and the White Castle is closed on Tuesdays.

It was starting to dawn on me that if a place was closed on one day a week, or one day a month, or even one day a year, that would be the day on which I approached it.

Still, it's an interesting defensive tactic and I couldn't help wondering if Monmouth Castle might have sustained less damage if its defenders had simply put up a sign pointing out to would-be attackers that they were closed on Tuesdays.

Even from outside its grounds, I could see that the White Castle was impressive. It derives its name from the whitewash, now long-weathered away, which was applied to its outer walls a hundred years after it was built. Painted white and sited in an imposing location, it must have presented a very visible sign of military strength and political power. Together with two other castles, it controlled traffic to and from Wales along the Monnow valley, but as the border became more peaceful its importance declined and it was abandoned by the mid-1500s.

An unusual claim to fame is that it was the subject of landscape paintings by Hitler's Deputy Fuhrer, Rudolf Hess, when he was held prisoner in the area during the Second World War.

Frustrated in my attempt to get a better look at the castle, I dropped down the hill a little and walked on until I found a good spot to camp. Sheltered from the wind by a hedge and out of the sight of walkers and landowners, I ate my dinner in the early evening sunshine and thought about my next day's walk.

I'd walked 33km today and I planned a shorter day for tomorrow. Hay-on-Wye was 26km away so, at my current rate of progress, I should make it in a day, with time to spare. I quite liked that "time to spare". I knew there was a campsite in Hay, and I was looking forward to a shower and a chance to wash some clothes. If the good weather held, I might even have time to catch the last of the sunshine and get them dry.

The sky stayed bright and clear, auguring a cold night ahead. I made sure I had enough layers on, took a nip of sloe gin from my hip flask and burrowed down into my sleeping bag, woolly hat close at hand in case I got cold in the night.

When I'm out walking in the summer, I tend to wake up when the sun comes up and go to bed when it gets dark. I went to bed at about 9pm, a time also known as "hiker midnight", and I was awoken the next day by a very raucous dawn chorus at 5am. I'd spent a warm, comfortable night, but when I opened the tent flap I saw traces of frost on the grass, so I had breakfast in bed to keep warm.

My morning walk to the village of Pandy was an enjoyable ramble across mostly-empty dairy fields. I was getting used to walking with wet feet each morning, as the dew in the fields soaked its way into my trail shoes. The morning routine, I'd deduced, was, for the first hour, cold, wet feet. For the second hour each morning my feet were warm and wet, and after that I ceased to care. The beauty of walking in trail shoes is that my feet might get wet quickly, but they dry quickly too, something I was never able to achieve in boots. I've walked hundreds of miles without a single blister since I made the transition.

I walked uphill through a cow pasture to the ancient church of St Cadoc's at Llangattock Lingoed. I could see the whitewashed church ahead of me through the trees, but between me and the gate which led into the churchyard was a large herd of cows, about a third of which were very young calves.

I've never been threatened by cattle, but any animal can get a touch defensive if they perceive their young as being in danger, so I made a wide detour around the herd, talking softly to them as I went. They stood and watched me with silent concentration, until I was out of their field.

At Pandy, I knew I'd pass the Lancaster Arms pub, so I was travelling light, intending to load up with water at the pub as I passed it. My cunning plan was scuppered by the fact that the pub had closed down and was now a bed and breakfast establishment.

It was still a little early to be knocking on doors and asking for water, so instead I strolled down the road to The Rising Sun and watered-up at the tap on the very agreeable campsite there.

Suitably replenished, it was time to start climbing Hattervel Hill, a mere hummock at 531m, but with steep slopes.

The clouds, wispy and high in the early morning, had moved off to the south and I was walking northwards under a clear sky. I felt the strength of the sun through my shirt on my arms and shoulders, and paused to put on thin gloves to protect the backs of my hands. I ground my way slowly uphill and it wasn't long before I topped out.

I found myself on a long ridge. I was on the eastern edge of the Black Mountains and the ridge twisted and turned as it stretched northwards under a clear sky, away from me towards Hay-on-Wye, out of sight in the distance. The border runs along this same ridge so as I strode along the broad path on its crest, I could look left into Wales or right into England, my home.

As I walked, the clouds came back, fluffy little cumulus this time, only a little higher than the hilltops, scudding across the bright blue sky from Wales towards England.

I made good time and just after lunchtime I dropped down into a hollow behind some rocks to get out of the wind and have something to eat.

I'd only been there a few minutes when I was joined by three lads with large rucksacks who were walking the same trail as I was. We chatted as we ate, and I discovered that their home town was Prestatyn, the northern terminus of the walk. They had got themselves to Chepstow and were now walking home, which must have put a different gloss on the walk for them. They had started off by camping but found they couldn't carry all the kit they thought they needed, so they'd posted most it home and carried on, staying in hotels and hostels instead of under canvas.

Even after that experience, their rucksacks were still bigger than mine. I sometimes wonder what it will take to persuade people to go lightweight. Neither logic nor emotion seem to sway them, that's for sure.

I finished first, so I wished my new friends good luck, shouldered my pack and set off again.

There was little water evident along the top of the ridge and I was glad I'd loaded up at Pandy. What felt like a long, hot slog saw me cross what would be the highest point of the trail at 703m, just before Hay Bluff, and then I was downhilling across the fields towards Hay-on-Wye, the already short grass worn down by many walkers and showing me the path very clearly.

It's my experience that the most difficult places to navigate through aren't wild places or town centres. Rather, the sticky bit tends to be that transition zone where the town meets the country. It's not difficult to find your way when you can pick out the hills and the valleys, or when you're following streets and town squares, but the way never seems quite so obvious in the fringe area where rural footpaths meet suburbia. I don't often get lost or take a wrong path, but when I do it's nearly always as I'm entering or leaving a town or a village.

I compensate for this by taking extra care over navigation as I go into or come out of towns, so on the edge of Hay I stopped to check my map. As I did so another walker came up behind me and asked if I was walking the Offa's Dyke Path. He was camping at the campsite in Hay and day-walking. We fell into step across the last few fields and he kindly showed me where the campsite was, on the other side of the town.

I was feeling pretty chipper after a shower, so I set my newly washed shirt and socks to dry on the campsite washing line and headed into Hay-on-Wye in search of food. Paul, my fellow camper, joined me for a drink and we talked backpacking over a few pints at The Blue Boar.

Hay-on-Wye is a nice little town. It's known principally for its bookshops and its annual festival but, like most towns along the English-Welsh border, it has plenty of history too. And it has two Norman castles, rather than one like other towns, although there isn't much left of either of them in Hay.

Hay-on-Wye was also home to Herbert Rowse Armstrong, a man who holds the unfortunate distinction of being the only British lawyer ever to have been hanged for murder. Armstrong was alleged to have poisoned both his wife and his business partner, and he was executed at Gloucester Prison in 1922.

It was just starting to get dark as Paul and I wended our way back to the campsite, still talking about our hobby. Paul told me that rain was forecast from 11 o'clock the next morning. "You'll be all right", he added, aware of my habit of making an early start, "It's always nicer packing up if it's not raining. You'll be able to pack up while it's still dry and you'll be miles away by the time the rain starts".

Comfortably set up on the campsite, I had no plans to hurry away the next morning. But maybe he was right, I thought. Maybe, with bad weather coming in, I should make an early start tomorrow. An accomplished sky-watcher by now, I decided to check the weather when I woke up early the next morning. Then I'd get moving, or not, depending on how I felt and what the weather looked like.

I woke at 5am, still warm and snug in my sleeping bag. I was so comfortable that I was very tempted to linger a little longer, but then I remembered the forecast and my resolution to check the weather.

I couldn't hear rain, and the tent was still and dark, so I was expecting to find the weather cloudy but not problematic. I unzipped the tent and leaned out.

The first thing I noticed was that the air outside was colder, a lot colder, than that inside my little hiking tent. The next was the big, black clouds, very low in the sky, racing across from the west like long, dark streamers.

The bad weather was here and it looked as if it would get worse before it got better.

Paul's piece of wisdom about striking camp before the rain flashed into my mind and I leapt out of bed as if galvanised. In a few minutes I was fed, clothed, packed and on my way.

I passed Paul's tent, still closed up and in darkness, but he was happily immune to the weather: he had another day to spend in Hay and a car to drive home in, and all the kit and spare clothes he could cram into that car.

I strode down the hill to the bridge over the Wye, mentally daring the weather to do its worst. I was well-equipped and dressed for what was coming, and I had enough food and water. What else could I need? I knew I'd get wet in prolonged bad weather, that much is always certain, but I had the kit and the attitude to carry on. "Bring it!" I thought to myself. "Bring it or stop threatening."

Just before the bridge I turned onto the riverside path and followed it alongside the Wye, and then across and around fields, the grass still dry this morning. I had the world to myself.

I bade the river a silent goodbye. It had been my companion and a staunch navigational handrail for most of my trip thus far, and I wouldn't see it again. I decided I liked the Wye.

The weather was so ominous, so close to bad, that I didn't think it possible it could get any more threatening. The next step would have to be cold and heavy rain, I concluded.

As if to show its power and my insignificance, the clouds darkened even more and the wind increased. Still no rain. It was like a winter's evening.

At three minutes to eleven, the wind started to whip a fine drizzle into my face. It was so close to what Paul had predicted that I couldn't escape a sneaking feeling that he must have had something to do with it.

This was good, persistent drizzle, slowly thickening, blown hard by the wind. I started up Disgwylfa Hill, the wind increasing in strength as I got higher.

Confronted with place names or personal names which look like unusual arrangements of letters, English people will often murmur, "I wonder what that's worth at Scrabble". In the case of Disgwylfa Hill, I can save you the trouble: it's worth 27 points, assuming no doubling or tripling.

Chapter 3

Into the Radnorshire Hills

I felt very alone and very small as I crossed Disgwylfa Hill in the wind and the rain. I knew I wouldn't be on it for very long, but I also knew that the next hill, Hergest Ridge, was higher and longer, giving the weather a bigger stage on which to play.

Soon I was down and crossing fields again, on my way to Gladestry and the route up Hergest. Surely, I felt, I should have met someone by now? Even the bed and breakfast crowd should be out on the trail by this time, I felt.

The thought was no sooner in my head than I spotted two figures in the far distance, smothered in waterproofs and walking towards me. We passed each other in the middle of a field, surrounded by sheep. The two men were middle-aged bed-and-breakfasters, walking the trail southbound. They hadn't long left their last overnight stop, but already they were soaked. They were cheerful though, and as they wiped the rain off their glasses and put them back on, we exchanged superlatives about the trail and swearwords about the weather.

I was under no illusions about the weather in this part of the world. Years ago, I'd spent a weekend walking in hills near here, and I'd started and finished at Gladestry, just up the road from where I was now standing. That had been in high summer, but it had provided a good example of how the weather can change and how unseasonal it can sometimes be. We'd started with baking summer sunshine and finished the walk in fog and such heavy rain that some of the roads had flooded.

When I reached it, Gladestry was still and quiet under the dark sky. So quiet that I couldn't entirely shake off the feeling that some colossal catastrophe had wiped out all of human civilisation while I'd been walking. As I marched through the silent village, a sign outside the church caught my eye. "Open for tea and coffee", it said, "All welcome".

That was all the persuasion I needed, and I was quickly through the gate and inside the church. The force of a habit inculcated long, long ago causing me to snatch my hat from my head as I entered.

Inside, I found everything I needed to make tea and coffee, with a note telling me that the church provided this for walkers. I admired both their charity and their business acumen. While the kettle was boiling I dug my wallet from its waterproof bag and left a donation, then made myself a coffee. When I emerged twenty minutes later I felt like a new man.

I made my way up Hergest Ridge through the rain, the grey gloom drawing in as I gained height. The path was easy to follow, but up on top the rain was driving horizontally and I was soon wet through, despite my waterproofs. I'd expected that, and I knew the key to avoiding hypothermia was to keep warm, so I had all my layers on and I worked to keep my core temperature up by walking, and by doing so determinedly, whether the path took me up or down.

I paused to check my bearings on the map, blowing rain off my upper lip as I did so. I was on course.

I angled the map to let the rainwater run off, re-folded it and put it away. There was supposed to be an old Victorian racecourse up here, but I couldn't see any sign of it. Mind you, in that weather you could have held a full-on race meeting right in front of me and I could easily have missed it.

Hergest Ridge is famous as the inspiration for Mike Oldfield's album of the same name, released in 1974. I remembered his earlier album, Tubular Bells, but I couldn't remember anything about the Hergest Ridge one. I looked around me. If Oldfield drew his inspiration from the real Hergest Ridge, most of his music must have been about being wet through, with occasional tracks majoring on how your clothes chafe you when they're really wet.

I smiled and blew more rain from my face. I wasn't far from Kington. In Kington I would have choices. There were pubs and cafés in Kington. I could use the campsite on the edge of town, or opt for a night in brick, if I wished and if I could find somewhere with a vacancy. In Kington I was to pick up my first food parcel from the Post Office, posted *poste restante* before I left home. I was wet through but feeling good as I passed the small stand of monkey puzzle trees[3] on

---

[3] *Monkey puzzle trees (*Araucaria araucana*) were brought to Britain from South America in 1795 by Archibald Menzies, botanist and surgeon to George Vancouver's circumnavigation of the world. Menzies attended a dinner hosted by the governor of Chile, at which some seeds of the monkey puzzle tree were served as dessert. Menzies trousered a handful of seeds and grew five young trees on the voyage home to England. Fifty years later the trees were still a rarity and had no common name, but in 1850, when barrister Charles Austin was shown one by a proud garden owner*

the top of the ridge and started down towards the town.

As I left the exposed hill, my path took me through pine trees and the wind dropped as I entered them. Without the wind chilling me, I began to warm up a little more, despite the hard rain.

The dirt track under my feet changed to gravel, and then to tarmac, giving me the distinct impression that I was regaining civilisation.

The woodland on my right gave way to a cultivated hedge. Beyond the hedge I saw two elderly ladies in a formal garden, underneath umbrellas, with coats buttoned up to the neck, wandering slowly through the driving rain. It looked a very English scene.

A few metres further on was a large car and coach park. It was occupied by one solitary coach which was full of elderly women. My heart went out to them! They had made time and travelled miles to see the gardens, only to have their day ruined by the weather. It really was a shame.

It was one o'clock as I entered the outskirts of the town and as I walked in, I started planning my campaign on Kington.

First, I decided, I would have lunch in a pub. Ideally a pub with a nice open fire. A large lunch, with beer, letting my clothes dry out while I was eating.

Next, I'd find somewhere to stay overnight. I wasn't sure what was available in the way of accommodation, but I'd worked out my priorities: I had camped for a few nights and

---

in Cornwall, he commented, "It would puzzle a monkey to climb that", and the name stuck.

I'd made good time through bad weather, so I decided I'd reward myself with a night in a B&B or a pub, if I could find somewhere. Failing that, I'd head for the campsite and get myself organised there.

That done, I'd find a coffee shop, relax and check my text messages. Then, when I'd updated my friends and family, I'd call at the post office and collect my food parcel. With all of that accomplished, I felt I'd be well set up for the next few days.

The first pub I saw as I entered Kington was the Royal Oak Inn. The fact that it was an inn suggested it would meet most of my criteria, so I headed straight for it to get food and accommodation[4].

As I entered the inn, I saw a notice pinned to the door stating that they only served food on Fridays and at weekends. That threw me for a second, because I honestly could not remember what day of the week it was. I paused in the doorway. I knew it wasn't a weekend. Was it a Friday? I rather thought not, but I wasn't sure. I decided the best approach was bluff, so I went up to the bar and asked if I could see the lunch menu.

The lady behind the bar told me she was sorry, but they only did lunch on Fridays. I pointed out that it was Friday, but she had it on good information that it was Thursday. Chef wasn't in on Thursdays.

Chef? Christ on a bike, I only wanted something with chips! I thanked her and crossed the road to The Swan.

---

[4] *Traditionally, an "inn" is a pub which also offers accommodation. Unfortunately many inns have ceased to provide beds but still call themselves inns, which can be confusing.*

The staff at The Swan were far more helpful. I like to think that my pre-pub ritual might have helped here. I forgot to apply it before entering the Royal Oak and it does make a difference.

Although I try to keep standards up, I have to admit I don't always look my best on the trail. Long days of walking, camping at night and the occasional total immersion by rain, all combine to ill-effect. Fatigued and unshaven, hair sticking up all over the place, and with an intense expression because of my total focus on forward progress, I'd find it difficult to argue with you if you were to describe me as looking like a rather tired axe-murderer. When I arrive at civilisation, I try to mitigate this look by brushing back my hair with my fingers, not thinking about axe-murdering and, well, that's it really. Outside The Swan I made an extra effort and removed my waterproofs.

Inside The Swan, the barmaid fussed around me, found me a table, took my order and hung my jacket and over-trousers up to dry. I got warm again, dried out somewhat, and enjoyed a cooked lunch. Only afterwards did I discover the pub has a separate entrance for muddy hikers like me, on the other side of the building.

They looked after me well at The Swan, and I was in good spirits as I put my dry waterproofs back on and walked into the town centre.

On an impulse, I walked into a hotel to ask about vacancies and found they had one room left. I snapped it up. It would, I felt, be prudent to base myself somewhere I could get my kit dry and boatload the calories that evening and the next morning, to prepare myself for the next leg of my journey.

I unpacked, hung a few things up and took a shower.

Suitably refreshed and reinvigorated, I left the hotel for the coffee shop opposite.

I was half-way across the high street when I had a change of heart. I could get coffee anytime, I decided, but I really should collect my food parcel. I had my passport with me as photo-identification, so it was with a warm, virtuous feeling, because I was removing a job from my "To Do" list, that I turned right and headed towards the post office.

The post office in Kington had two serving positions, both of them staffed, and I queued to be served at one of them.

When my turn came, the woman behind the counter smiled helpfully at me.

"What can I do for you?"

I held out my passport and said, "I'm here to collect a parcel, posted *poste restante*. It's in the name of John Davison."

The woman ignored my proffered passport and spoke as one might to a small child.

"Do you have the card the postman left?"

She obviously thought I was trying to collect a parcel which the post office had tried to deliver to my home while I was out.

I shook my head. "There's no card. This isn't an attempted delivery at my house. I'm calling to collect a *poste restante* parcel, addressed to me at this post office."

She professed never to have heard of, "Poste...what was it?", and looked to her co-worker, although whether for enlightenment or support I couldn't tell.

I explained what *poste restante* is, while the counter lady stared back at me blankly. When I'd finished, she looked sideways at her colleague and said, "Well, I've never heard of that before. Have you?"

With that deliberate, irritating slowness that only comes from years of working in a post office, her friend finished serving the customer she was dealing with. The customer left and silence fell. She carefully tucked a small piece of paper into a drawer under the counter, then wrapped an elastic band around something and put that into the same drawer. She closed the drawer. Then she looked at me.

"What is it again?"

I took a deep breath and explained for a second time how *poste restante* works: that I simply address a piece of mail to my name and this post office, and then call in with photographic identification to prove who I am when I collect it.

As I explained it, my mind raced to work out what I'd do if they didn't have my food parcel, how I might solve this surprise conundrum and continue my journey. I didn't make any progress on that one, because my head was swimming with the surreal absurdity of the situation I found myself in. Me, explaining a basic post office service to post office staff who should have known it better than I did. At one point while I was talking I found myself looking around for confirmation that I was actually in a post office, that I hadn't strayed into, say, a pharmacist or a bank by mistake.

The process should be straightforward and I found that I wanted to shout at them. I wanted to ask them what the hell they were thinking, working in a post office, actually on the bloody payroll of the place, when they'd never heard of *poste restante.* I wanted to tell them that the system had been working ever since Rowland Hill sold the first Penny Black stamp in 1840 and that it's listed on the post office website. I wanted to ask them whether they'd heard of other aspects of postal work, like letters and stamps, and offer to explain those concepts to them as well.

But I didn't.

When I'd finished, both women looked at me and one of them folded her arms. They were too polite to say it, but their body language was clear: he's making it up.

I could have pointed out that if I wanted to play practical jokes on post office staff, I could have done so in my home town, without the need to carry a rucksack across sixty miles of open country in all weathers beforehand.

But I didn't.

I tried to remember whether I'd gone through my pre-pub routine, to look less wild and scary before I entered the post office, but then I remembered that I'd just showered and changed, so my current look was as good as I was going to get.

I tried a different tack and told them about my journey, and how I had posted food parcels ahead to collect at post offices. I'd been doing it for years I told them, and it had always worked before.

Like the English legal system, the two post office ladies relied heavily upon precedent. As soon as I mentioned that I'd been posting parcels to myself at post offices for years with nary a problem, they perked up, and one of them said she'd take a look "out the back". A quote from Oliver Hardy flew, unasked for, into my head: "Now we're getting someplace!"

There were no other customers, so I chatted with my server's friend while she was gone. After an interval of a few minutes she returned, but not with a parcel. I prevailed upon her to take a second look and, sportingly, she did so, but the result was the same.

Both ladies now seemed to perceive me more as a victim of circumstance than as the nuisance I'd been only a few minutes before, and they started to make well-intentioned but unhelpful suggestions. They asked if I had the tracking number for the parcel.

They meant well, but I had to pour cold water on that idea. It would be of no help to find out where the parcel was: the problem was that it wasn't in Kington.

I thanked the two ladies and wandered out of the post office and back into the rain, deep in thought. "Panic slowly" is a good maxim in these situations, so I headed for the coffee shop to think through my options.

I could try again at the post office tomorrow morning, although the fact that Kington post office didn't operate *poste restante* did not bode well, and I didn't have any confidence that my parcel might appear there overnight.

I could press on with my journey and feed myself from pubs and corner shops. I took my map and my data sheet out of my pocket and checked the likely locations of food sources. There weren't many of them, but a bigger problem with that approach was my stove.

My camping stove is small, light and boils water very, very quickly. That's fine for the type of food I'd sent ahead in parcels, but no use for anything else. Food requiring even a short simmer would simply be burned straight onto the pan. So the stove would be dead weight for the rest of the walk and heating anything other than the occasional drink would be impossible.

Did I fancy living on corner-shop sandwiches, supplemented by the occasional pub meal and nothing else? In all honesty, I didn't. But even that approach would necessitate altering my schedule so as to pass pubs when they were open and serving food.

Could I make it to my second food parcel? Possibly, if I didn't mind roughing it in terms of menu. But after the fiasco in Kington, I had no confidence that my second food parcel would have been delivered, and I realised why I'd thought of Laurel and Hardy back in the post office.

I sipped my coffee and allowed myself the luxury of a few moments of recrimination. I'd paid a lot of money to post my food parcels, with delivery guaranteed within 48 hours, but it looked as if the delivery company, Parcelforce, couldn't be relied upon to carry out a task as simple as delivering a parcel to a post office.

Back to the problem at hand. I got out a notebook and pen, and started jotting down options, playing about with them on paper.

Ten minutes later, I'd finished my coffee and an Eccles cake, but I was no further forward on my walk to Prestatyn.

It was about that time that another thought came into my head: I do this stuff for fun, because I enjoy it. I scanned the notes I'd made. None of my options, nor any permutation of them, looked like fun.

The best option seemed to be going home, reorganising

myself and coming back. That idea smacked of giving up, of hoisting the white flag, and I've never done that on a long walk before, so I went back to my notes and tried to make the alternatives look better.

But they didn't look better.

Reluctant to make the decision too quickly, I took my crockery to the counter and shouted a "Thank you" through to the kitchen where the coffee shop staff were washing up. I stepped outside into the rain and crossed the road, back to my hotel. As I did so I noticed that the skies were a dark black, as if to reflect my mood.

Back in my hotel room I watched the news on television and then looked through my notes again. The central decision seemed to be whether I wanted to tough it out and finish this walk in one go, or whether I wanted to enjoy it. I reached for the phone and booked a cab to the nearest railway station for tomorrow morning.

---------- XXX ----------

A week later the same cab driver picked me up from the same station and dropped me back in Kington.

My food strategy was now geared up for corner shops. I had a different stove and pot, a pot cosy and a plan to live off of the rubbish that small grocery shops sell and which is easily prepared on the trail: instant noodles, instant pasta, chocolate bars, cereal bars and pop tarts. The sort of stuff that I normally wouldn't touch with a ten foot pole. But I was confident that I could acquire it, prepare it, and that it would get me to Prestatyn.

I set my tent up on the campsite in Kington, in the lee of a tall hedge to protect me from the wind which was gusting across the site.

It felt good to be back, even if I did have a nagging feeling that I'd been demoted from a thru-hiker to a section-hiker[5].

I knocked up dinner, did some stretches against the wall of the toilet block and then took an evening stroll around Kington.

Kington isn't a big town. In many parts off the country it wouldn't be regarded as a town at all, maybe just a large village, but it was clearly a town in spirit and in aspiration. Its high street contained a range of shops and services beyond those usually found in such a small place. I wondered how most of them managed to survive, and the occasional derelict shop front reminded me that not all of them did.

I dallied by the River Arrow, but there wasn't much to see, so I checked my map and made my way back up the hill to reconnoitre the early stages of tomorrow's walk.

Like, it seems, every other town along the English-Welsh border, the Normans built a castle at Kington. Unlike most of the other towns, very little of Kington's castle remains: it was totally destroyed by King John in 1216.

The area around Kington is said to be haunted by the Black Dog of Hergest, the sight of which is supposed to be a

---

[5] *"Thru-hiker" and "section-hiker" are American terms. A thru-hiker is someone who hikes a trail from beginning to end in one go; a section-hiker hikes the same trail, but in discrete segments rather than as one continuous journey.*

warning of impending death. Sir Arthur Conan Doyle, author of the Sherlock Homes stories, stayed nearby just a short while before he wrote *The Hound of the Baskervilles*, and the Black Dog of Hergest is popularly supposed to have been his inspiration for Sherlock Holmes' "gigantic hound".

A notice on the park gate reminded dog owners that dogs can't pick up their own faeces, and implored them to clear up after their dumb chums. Black Dogs of Hergest be warned: Middle England is fine with harbingers of death, as long as they don't crap everywhere.

Chapter 4

The Shropshire Hills and the Plain of Montgomery

Walking again!

I was so eager to get started that I was up and on the trail by 6am. The high, grey clouds whipping across the sky suggested that last night's high winds were still in evidence, albeit at higher elevations.

I started by wearing all my layers of clothing as defence against the early morning chill. Walking makes you warm, so I knew it wouldn't be long before I'd have to stop and remove them. I'd read Ranulph Fiennes' account of trekking across Antarctica, in which he describes walking across the ice in a vest and trousers because of the body heat he was generating, so I was confident I'd warm up.

As the morning developed, so did the weather, and it wasn't long before I found myself in perfect walking weather: warm and sunny, with a cooling breeze.

On the hills before Knighton I met a party of seven. Five of them were from Seattle, Washington, and two were from

Shropshire in England, all of them walking the Offa's Dyke Path from north to south. They had much experience of British trails and I regretted my inexperience of American hiking. I made a mental note to do some research when I got home, and maybe even go there to hike, if I can get a permit to camp in the national parks[6].

I arrived at Knighton just before lunchtime. I'd put 21km on the clock, but I felt up for it and I was keen to do more. A brief refuelling stop, I thought, and then move on again.

I bought a packet of sandwiches from a shop on the main drag and ate them sitting on a bench in the shade. When I'd finished, I crumpled up the packet and put it in a nearby bin. I quite fancied a coffee, I thought to myself, but I didn't fancy unpacking my kit and brewing up on Knighton high street.

Some walkers are fond of saying, "The trail will provide", and, as if to prove the truth of this aphorism, right opposite the bin was a coffee shop. It would be wrong, I felt, to pass this up.

Getting the miles under your trail shoes can burn a lot of calories. Even if I eat like a pig, I usually lose weight on a long walk, so I've got used to treating long-distance walking as a licence to eat pretty much anything I choose whenever I feel like it. Once inside the coffee shop, my reasoning ran like this:

I've just had lunch but I'm still hungry.

---

[6] *No easy matter from 5,000 miles away: my attempt to hike the John Muir Trail in California was stymied by the need to acquire a permit and the sheer difficulty of doing so.*

I know I need to keep my calories up on a long walk.

What's the most calorie-dense food?

Why, fat, of course. It has 9 calories per gram, compared to 4 calories per gram for protein and carbohydrate.

So I walked up to the counter, and ordered a coffee and the biggest chocolate cream bun they had in the place. At this point I'll draw a discreet veil over the feeding frenzy that followed; I'll just say that I don't think I've ever enjoyed an item of food so much.

The town of Knighton sits in a deep vale, surrounded by hills. It's on the River Teme and it has the distinction of being located in Wales, but its railway station is in England. The name "Knighton" means "town of the knights", a reference to Knighton's two motte-and-bailey castles, which reveal the town's status as a border town, where knights protected from Welsh incursions. The Welsh name for the town is more prosaic, Tref-y-clawdd, which translates as "town on the dyke".

Knighton has one of only two churches in Wales which are dedicated to St Edward, the patron saint of England before St George took over the role in 1350. Knighton is also home to the Offa's Dyke Centre.

The Offa's Dyke Centre is the base of the Offa's Dyke Association, a charity which promotes and protects both the dyke and the Offa's Dyke Path. The Centre is a modern building on the north edge of Knighton, but although it's modern, the Centre does look as if it's seen better days and the toilets, I found, are a disgrace.

Inside, the Centre had displays about the dyke and the

history of the area. The displays explained that the origins of the dyke are not known and in consequence many of its aspects are speculated about rather than fully understood. Work on the dyke is thought to have started in 785CE and probably finished just a few years later. Despite the tremendous effort which must have gone into building it, we still don't know if it was intended for defence, as a boundary or to overawe potential opposition.

I'm not sure what "protecting the dyke" amounts to in practice, and the Centre didn't give much away. I had encountered occasional exhortations to not walk on the dyke, which struck me as odd when farmers drive heavy machinery over it every day, and even through it in some places. Cattle and sheep wear tracks across and around it, and badgers, foxes and rabbits burrow into it. But only walkers are kept off of it, probably because we're the only users of the dyke who will respond to a polite request. And the Association has to start somewhere, I suppose.

Fuelled by my recent huge calorie intake, I strolled out of Knighton, across the railway line and up the hill.

I knew that the next 25km or so, known locally as "The Switchbacks", are considered to be the toughest part of the trail. The term "switchbacks" suggested to me a path that zigzags on a hillside in order to gain or lose height, but I was to find that my impression was mistaken. I'd walked up switchback paths in the Alps and I felt that I had an idea of what to expect. I was wrong.

North of Knighton, up until Brompton Cross, the path runs in pretty much a straight line. The term, "The Switchbacks", refers simply to the repetitive, and steep, up-and-down nature of the route. Up and down like a rollercoaster ride, but with no motive power other than your own two legs. The only way through, I decided, was to grit my teeth (metaphorically, of course) and to keep walking, pausing occasionally for breath and to enjoy the astounding scenery.

In pure tourist terms, there isn't much to see on this stretch, as the path drops downhill then rears back up again. And again. And again.

Not much to see, but plenty to enjoy. There's the feeling of peace, the tranquillity of the quiet little valleys, the stillness and the greenness of it all, the sheer pleasure and privilege of being amongst it.

The dyke is much in evidence after Knighton and its regained presence felt almost as if I was walking with an old friend after a long time apart. I strode along it, wondering about the people who had walked on it before me in the 1,200 years since it was built.

I was aiming for Springhill Farm. I knew there was a campsite on the farm and that, by the time I got there, I'd total 31km walked for the day – a tidy distance in my terms.

I approached the farm up a lane. As I got close to the farmyard entrance, a tatty old border collie came racing across the farmyard, straight towards me. I raised my trekking poles and prepared to sell my life dearly. Confronted with the trekking pole points, she stopped in the wide-open gateway, at the fence-line, and barked and snarled at me.

Her barking set off all the other dogs in the farmyard and, from the noise they made, there seemed to be many of them, but none came out to join her.

I edged cautiously past the black and white fury in the farmyard gateway and walked further up the lane. I anticipated an attack from the rear, but none came and the collie stayed where she was, still barking, and watching me closely.

A small gate from the lane gave into the front garden of the farmhouse. I checked that no dogs had access and let myself through the gate, into the little garden. The farmhouse stood silent in front of me. I stepped into the small porch and rang the two bells next to the front door. Then I used the door knocker. The only response I got was when the second bell sounded loudly inside the house and set the dogs off again in the farmyard on the other side.

The dogs subsided and I considered my options. A sign on the lane confirmed that the farm allowed camping. I took my rucksack off and set it on an ornamental bench in the front garden, then I walked around the side of the farmhouse to see if the campsite might be behind it.

I didn't find the campsite, but I did find another border collie, younger and more aggressive than the one I'd encountered in the farmyard. Luckily for me this dog was attached to one end of a piece of blue baler twine and the other end of the twine was attached to something heavy and solid. The dog made it very plain that he would have given up his kin and his birthright for just two minutes of mixing it with me. I didn't want to find out what the breaking strain of the baler twine was, so I beat a hasty retreat back to the front garden.

Here, I noticed the camping sign had a phone number on it, so I quickly fished my mobile phone out of my pack and dialled the number. As I pressed "dial" I mentally kicked myself: surely the phone number on the sign would be the landline inside the empty house? A split second later my thought was confirmed as the telephone rang, unanswered, in the farmhouse, setting all the dogs barking again as it did so.

I was getting fed up with this, I decided. I looked around for a tap to fill my water bottles so that I could move on and wild camp. Just at that moment I heard a footstep on gravel, coming from behind a barn, over in the farmyard. I shouted, he shouted back, and eventually we managed to cross paths.

He was a youngish chap, in his early 20s I'd guess, and he told me that yes, they did allow camping on the farm. He gestured towards a large, empty field of long grass on the other side of the farmhouse and offered to show me "the facilities".

The facilities consisted mostly of a small, modern kitchen, toilet and shower, all in need of a good clean and seemingly used mainly for the storage of empty cider cans. I stuck my head into the shower and made approving noises while my host scooped the empty cans into a bin bag. I paid him for one night and he left me to my own devices.

My first thought was to boil one of the two kettles and make myself a cup of tea. Then, I decided, I'd put the tent up, wash myself and my clothes, and get dinner, in whichever order seemed most efficient to me while I was drinking my tea.

It was a few minutes before I realised that nothing was happening. A quick check revealed that this was because the kettle was broken. I filled the second kettle, but that was no better. I filled my water bottles and decided to put the tent up and have tea there.

I stepped out of the kitchen into the back garden of the farmhouse and the collie on the blue twine flew at me. The string snapped as if it wasn't there and the dog was on me.

I gripped my water bottle with one hand and laid about me

mightily with my trekking pole in the other, intent on hurting the dog as much as I could before it got me, because its determination left me with no doubt that it would get me.

After what seemed like minutes of frantic barking, foul language and blurred movement, but was probably only a few seconds, I got out of the dog's sphere of influence unscathed and made it back to the camping field. I never went back to the "facilities" at Springhill Farm.

The next morning dawned bright and still and clear. I know that because I was up at dawn and back on the trail by 5am. High up, a few wisps of cirrus cloud decorated a sky that was duck egg blue, and a faint mist rose up from the dew. It was one of those early mornings that you look at and know it's going to be a scorcher.

I started down the first of that day's switchbacks, the farm dogs' barking getting fainter behind me until it petered out altogether. Sheep and their lambs stared at me, blinking uncomprehendingly, seemingly bewildered that anyone would be up at this hour, and in their field.

I made my first water point and "cameled up" by drinking a litre of water, as well as filling my bottle. The morning was completely still, the sun slowly climbing in the empty sky.

The many steep uphill sections were hard, but I kept moving and ground out the miles. At least, I pondered, there was no chance of me losing the trail: on the many uphill stretches it seemed to be about six inches in front of my nose.

As I walked, I pondered on Parcelforce, the incompetent sods who had so spectacularly failed to deliver my food parcels. When I'd contacted them to complain, a woman informed to me that, under their terms of carriage, an attempted delivery counted as an actual delivery. They had done their part, she assured me, and I was due no money back or compensation, even though my parcels had not been delivered.

This wilful perversion of the English language annoyed me almost as much as the fact that I'd paid for something I hadn't received. I wondered whether, if I was ever stupid enough to use their service again, they would accept no money, on the basis that an attempted payment was as good as an actual payment? Of course they wouldn't. So why do they expect it of their customers? And if you were a pregnant woman, would you regard an attempted delivery as meaning the same as an actual delivery? Of course not.

At 8 o'clock I stopped and went through what was becoming my mid-morning routine: snack, drink, factor 50 sun cream on face and neck, sun hat, light gloves, move on again. I found it pleasing that it had evolved into a procedure centred on sun protection and not rain protection.

I passed Brompton Cross in good spirits, partly because I was making good time and partly because I knew it marked the end of The Switchbacks and that meant I would have some easier walking for a day or two.

I rounded a corner and at a stile in front of me I saw four young lads, stripped to the waist and carrying huge, army-style rucksacks.

In my experience, young people with ridiculously large rucksacks are almost always completing an aspect of their Duke of Edinburgh's Award Scheme, so when I asked them, "D of E?" I already knew the answer.

They confirmed that yes, they were school pupils completing

their Duke of Edinburgh's Award[7]. They were on their last day of walking and their target was Forden, about 8km away, where they would be picked up by minibus and taken home. They had started that day at Mellington Hall, 2km further back.

I know the D of E Scheme is very health and safety conscious, and very wary of legal action if anything were to go wrong. That fact was very evident as I hiked the next 8km to Forden, because I encountered the school minibus every time the path crossed a lane, its occupants checking on the well-being of their four charges. Those lads can't have walked more than three kilometres without meeting their teachers and the minibus.

I know too, that participants are required to carry a lot of "just in case" kit. But I couldn't help wondering whether they might enjoy the experience a whole lot more if they carried much less, and learned and applied more skills.

As I walked on across the flat Plain of Montgomery I found myself musing on whether their teachers might find it more rewarding too. After all, why teach a long out-of-date skillset when better alternatives are available? I doubted if they'd do the same in other subjects.

As if to emphasise my thoughts, a little further up the trail I stopped to chat with a man who was also walking the Offa's Dyke Path, in his case southbound. His pack was about the same size as mine but he was staying in bed and breakfast

---

[7] *The Duke of Edinburgh's Award Scheme is a youth improvement programme founded in 1956 by Prince Phillip, Duke of Edinburgh. Participants complete activities which involve volunteering, physical activity, practical and social skills, and expedition skills. The scheme started in the UK but now operates in 140 countries.*

establishments. He assumed I was doing the same as him and he was visibly surprised when I told him I was backpacking and camping. Didn't I feel I was cheating, he asked me, by having my baggage sent on ahead? I had to explain that nothing had been sent ahead, that I was carrying everything I needed, but he still felt the need to check off the larger items individually.

"Tent?"

"Yes."

"Sleeping bag?"

"Yes."

"Well, I never!"

I don't need validation from other hikers, but after that occasion I did walk on feeling that I was getting it right.

A little further up the trail I deviated through Lymore to get to the little town of Montgomery, to pick up something for lunch.

Montgomery took its name from the French lord who was given this area by William the Conqueror after the Norman Conquest. It contains a beautiful thirteenth century castle which was built by Henry III during his campaign against the Welsh prince, Llewellyn the Great. The castle saw action in the Civil War and, but you'll be way ahead of me by now, it was slighted when the war finished to remove its military value. Today it is a very atmospheric ruin.

Another interesting feature of Montgomery is the grave of John Davies in the churchyard of St Nicholas' Church. In 1821, Davies was convicted of robbery at Montgomery and sentenced to death by hanging. All through his trial and after he had been sentenced, Davies protested his innocence, stating that God would not allow grass to grow on his grave for a hundred years. As he predicted, no grass grew on his final resting place.

Personally, if I was about to be hanged for something I didn't do, I'd hope a merciful and all-powerful God might do a bit more for me than some after-the-event horticulture, but there we are. Anyway, despite the divine intervention, local people seem sceptical about Davies' innocence because the story is still known as "The Legend of the Robber's Grave".

Montgomery's main streets hold some beautiful Georgian buildings, which reflect the wealth and status of the place when it was the county town of Montgomeryshire and an important market. Like so many places on this walk, the town had an atmosphere of calm longevity. This, I felt, was a place I could come back to.

I sat on a bench in the main square and ate the sandwiches I had just purchased in the town shop, watching the quiet, measured daily life of Montgomery unfold in front of me. I could happily have tarried, but I remembered how uncomfortable the last ten kilometres had been the day before and I wanted to finish my work for the day before I rested.

I left the town on the main road, which was strangely quiet despite it being the middle of the day, crossed the bridge over a river too small to be named on my map but which nonetheless constituted the national boundary in these parts, and turned north onto the dyke once more.

I planned to reach The Green Dragon Inn at Buttington. I knew the Green Dragon had a campsite behind the main pub building, and the lure of a shower, hot food and decent beer was irresistible. It occurred to me that, so far on this trip, I had given precious little custom to the public house licensees along the Offa's Dyke Path and I intended to put that right without further ado. Rural pubs are going out of business left, right and centre, and I was determined to do my bit to stop the rot.

The beer/food/shower combination (see how these things automatically prioritise themselves if you let your subconscious do the work?) distracted me from my navigation and I got lost in the village of Kingswood before I realised where I'd missed my turning and found my way back to the path.

The flat bit was over for the day and I was soon ascending again, walking along gravel tracks through shady deciduous and conifer woodland. Presented with a large block of concrete by the side of the path, on a whim I sat down and checked my feet. I was surprised to see that they looked like the feet of a corpse which has spent too long immersed in a river. This was clearly a warning that I would be foolish to ignore, so I took some time out to wash my feet, dry them and then to dry my socks and shoes. Then I lightened my load by drinking a good portion of the water I was carrying.

Not long after my rest stop, I reached the Iron Age hillfort at Beacon Ring. I knew where I was because the two large radio masts on the hilltop left no doubt. I was intrigued, though, to find out what my map meant by the legend, "E.R. Memorial".

A large noticeboard revealed all. In 1953, when our current Queen was crowned, enthusiastic locals infilled the hillfort by planting trees in the area enclosed by the almost-circular earthworks. And not just any trees: they planted a mixture of conifers and deciduous trees so that, when seen from above, the plantation reads "E II R", the monogram of their new queen, Elizabeth II.

I was much taken with this idea, even though the result is only visible from the air. I was reminded of the trees planted near Amesbury on Salisbury Plain by a local landowner, which show the positions of the British and enemy ships at the Battle of the Nile in 1798. It seemed to me to be a long-lasting way to record an enthusiasm of its day, a simple emotion but nevertheless one strongly felt.

The current managers of the site, the Clwyd-Powys Archaeological Trust, do not share my enthusiasm however, and the information board sniffily notes that, "It is hoped to gradually manage the vegetation back to its former condition."

The hillfort at Beacon Ring was built in the Iron Age, between 600BCE and 50CE, and most of the timber on the surrounding hilltops would have been cleared in that era. They are still bare today. The fort is said to have been used by Cadwallon, the King of the Britons, in his battles with Edwin of Northumbria in 630CE. Another local legend says that the forces of Henry Tudor gathered near here in 1485, before marching to Bosworth Field and the battle which would make him King Henry VII and establish the Tudor dynasty on the throne of England for over a hundred years.

Chapter 5

The Severn Valley

The hillfort at Beacon Ring and its stand of trees would have made a very enjoyable overnight stopping place, but the siren call of the Green Dragon and the delights it offered was too strong, so I set off down the hill.

I was soon crossing the fields that separated me from Buttington, passing the industry park on the B4388 road, and there was The Green Dragon Inn, right in front of me at the T-junction.

I could almost taste the beer and food by that point. I'd even have a pudding, I decided.

As I got closer, I saw a large chalkboard in the car park which read:

WE ARE SORRY BUT
DUE TO OUR ANNUAL
PUB OUTING WE ARE
CLOSED
TODAY. OPEN AS
USUAL TOMORROW.

How's your luck?

I checked the door that led into the bars. Firmly closed, and the place was dark inside.

It was time for Plan B.

I wasn't quite sure what Plan B was. When I thought about it, it was a lot like Plan A but without the beer and food.

I found a spot on the campsite, a reasonable distance from the nearby "A" road and its traffic noise, and put the tent up with that quick, practised ease which you only acquire when you've been doing it every day for a while. Then I extracted my only set of spare clothes from their waterproof bag, rooted out my washing kit and headed for the shower.

I was pleased to find that even though the pub was shut, the shower and toilets were all still open and available to campers. I was the only person on the site with a tent, but there were several caravans and motor homes already there, and I guessed the outhouses had been left unlocked deliberately.

I stood in the shower and revelled in the hot water for almost a minute before washing my shirt, pants and socks. I rinsed them, also under the shower, and wrung them out, then put them off to one side, out of the way. Next, I got myself cleaned up.

Some campsites can be a touch condescending towards campers who want to dry laundry on their property, but there was no-one in at the Green Dragon to tell me off, so I hung my washing out to dry near my tent.

Food next.

If you're camping, a picnic table can offer a surprisingly high degree of luxury and convenience, because it makes a significant change from sitting on the ground or, if the weather's bad, from sitting cooped up in your tent.

There were no picnic tables in the camping field, but there were plenty of them in the pub's beer-garden. Normally they would be solely for patrons of the pub, but with no-one around to tell me otherwise, it made sense to use one, so I grabbed my stove and food, and chose a suitable spot.

If my dinner seemed a little sparse, well, that was because it suffered in comparison with a pub menu. I reconstituted some dried noodles, then stirred in a sachet of sardines in a rather lively sauce, which I'd bought under the mistaken impression they were tuna.

Pub menu staples such as steak and chips intruded, unasked for, into my mind, but I pushed them back out again and worked my way through my sardines and noodles. The best I can say about that dinner is that it filled a hole.

I made a mug of tea, opened a packet of digestive biscuits, and took a look around me. The Green Dragon is a seventeenth century building with outhouses that look very much as if they used to be stables. It is located on a main road and I wondered if it used to be a coaching inn.

I found myself looking towards the car park every time I heard a vehicle on the main road, in case the pub outing was returning. I'm not sure what form that would have taken, and I might be doing them an injustice, but a coach full of drunk people seemed the most likely occurrence.

My reveries were interrupted by a spot of rain and I remembered I had washing out. I grabbed up my things and headed back to my tent.

I slept well that night and rose the next morning at a time that was more civilised than it was "hiker". The inside of the pub building was still in darkness and there were no vehicles in the car park, so it looked as if the annual outing was an overnight affair.

I followed my usual practice and drank a litre of water before moving off. Some impulse made me check that I hadn't left anything in the shower-room nearby and, for the first time, I noticed a plug socket there.

I'd counted on being able to recharge my phone in the pub but the need had slipped my mind when I'd had to produce Plan B at short notice the evening before. I rely upon my phone to update the people who care about me and I didn't know when I'd get another chance to charge it, so I plugged it in and delayed my start by a further 45 minutes while it sucked in some power.

Eventually I was fed, watered and packed, and my phone was charged. There was still no sign of the Jolly Boys' outing, so I shouldered my pack and set off towards the River Severn, walking along the "A" road under a sky the colour of old pewter.

I crossed the Severn on a Victorian iron bridge, an experience made interesting by the coincidence of high-speed traffic and the lack of a footway. Against all the odds I found that I was still alive when I reached the other bank, so I stepped back from the traffic and pulled out my map.

The map told me I had to turn right almost immediately after the bridge and an Offa's Dyke Path sign on a post confirmed this. But the gate across the gravel driveway was very firmly padlocked shut. It was the first unopenable farm gate with no stile or foot-gate that I'd encountered on my walk.

Ahead of me, at the end of the driveway, was a dilapidated cottage. Outside the cottage I could see a pickup truck and what looked like men working, although I couldn't tell what they were doing.

I got the distinct impression that they didn't want anyone getting too close. After all, whatever they were doing, it hadn't been enough for them to close the gate – they had felt a need to lock it as well. And walkers would be passing through here most days, so they must have known it was part of a national footpath.

Wondering what sort of illegality I was about to stumble across, I made my way down the gravel drive.

There was no-one near the pick-up truck when I reached it. I walked around it towards the next gate, which also bore an Offa's Dyke Path marker. This gate was blocked up with a wooden pallet and I had to kick my way through it.

I emerged on the other side next to a barn, aware of a noise that sounded like machinery but of a type which I couldn't identify precisely. I rounded the barn and found that I was right in the middle of a hive of activity.

On my left was what looked like a black wooden wall about a metre and a half high but was, I noticed, the front of a large, raised stage. On the stage were four men in singlets and jeans. Sheep were being supplied to them one at a time through slots in the wall of a large shed that adjoined the back of the stage, and the men were shearing them, completely clearing them of fleece, in just a few seconds each. The finished sheep were bundled off the front of the stage and dropped back into the field which contained their fellows.

There was a lot of baa-ing going on and the sound was delicately different from that of a normal field of sheep. The shorn sheep stood about looking bewildered, surprised almost, as if they couldn't quite believe what had happened to them. The unshorn sheep were baa-ing mournfully, as if in sympathy with their processed colleagues, apparently unaware that they would be next.

I usually exchange at least a civil "good morning" with people I pass on the trail, but no-one involved in this operation would even make eye contact with me, so I turned and moved on.

Buttington is thought to be the place where, in 893CE, a combined Welsh and Mercian army defeated a Danish army which had marched from Essex and was thus a pivotal moment in the campaign against the Viking invasion. 893 sounds an awfully long time ago, but of course, Offa's Dyke was already old by then.

I was walking along the flood plain of the young River Severn. At Buttington it looked completely different from the wide tidal estuary where I'd started my walk at Sedbury Cliffs and I was struck, as I often have been before, by how unpleasant a river the Severn is. By that, I'm not referring to my surroundings, which were agreeable enough, but to the river itself.

I try to avoid anthropomorphism. I don't generally attribute "anger" to something which can't feel it, like bad weather or clouds. But whenever I encounter the River Severn I find words describing human emotions and intentions foremost in my mind.

On my few encounters with it, the Severn has impressed itself upon me as a vicious, malevolent river. As a child, I watched the Severn Bore bowl over my younger brother (he escaped unharmed), and as an adult I've seen the damage the Severn has inflicted on the town of Shrewsbury when it floods.

Here at Buttington, the Severn was aggressively incising itself deeper into the floodplain, filthy, chocolate-brown fast-swirling water undermining the banks at every bend and felling huge clods of earth and turf. The river's action was dark and striking, and its speed and intensity unexpected. It was almost as if I'd rounded a hedge in a thunderstorm and found a murder being committed in front of me.

I looked from the river across the field to the road I would soon cross, and in the distance a man was coming towards me. He turned out to be a southbounder from Canada. Like me he was walking the Offa's Dyke Path and camping, but he specialised in camping at bed and breakfast places, and at pubs. "If you ask them," he told me, "they usually have a little place where you can camp, often in the garden. It's a lot cheaper than bed and breakfast, and you still get to use the toilets and shower."

The clouds were beginning to lift. I crossed the road and stepped up onto the towpath of the Montgomery Canal.

Originally called the Montgomeryshire Canal, this canal may be unique in Britain, because it wasn't built so that its investors might make a profit by hauling goods. Instead, the plan was to transport lime which would be used to improve the farmland further up the valley. The profit would come, its backers hoped, not from the canal, but from the increased yields of that farmland.

The 53km canal was begun in 1794 and completed in 1821. 27 years! It works out at only 2km of canal constructed each year. They must have had faith in that farmland!

The canal became and stayed profitable, mainly because the railways arrived relatively late in the area, but it made losses after the First World War and closed in 1936. An Act of Parliament formally abandoned it in 1944.

I made good time along the flat towpath and I soon reached Pool Quay.

Pool Quay was not, as I'd initially thought, a product of the canal. It was so named because it was the highest navigable point on the River Severn and so it became the river quay for the nearby town of Welshpool ("Pool"). It was only later, when the canal came, that it also became the canal quay for Welshpool.

My path turned away from the canal at Pool Quay and I left it with reluctance. I enjoy canal walking. The going tends to be relatively easy, so I can cover a good distance, and I like the closeness of history, which is a part of any canal walk.

I followed the low-lying land by the side of the Severn, cutting straight across its meanders and stepping around the big, interlocked heaps of driftwood, still piled up from the last floods. The sky was blue now, and the sun was out. I walked through cow pastures yellow with buttercups, feeling a growing sense of entitlement as I did so. Dammit, I deserved a day of good weather after that rain before Kington!

I was alone with my thoughts for mile after mile. The great walker and writer, John Hillaby, called this phenomenon "skull cinema", a flow of thoughts, often very personal thoughts, which can't always be turned off and which, if not attended to, "can become morbid and follow patterns of discontent".

I couldn't deflect or break my train of thought and, as I paced along, I thought through some of the most difficult experiences of my life. I was close to tears at one point.

Eventually, I managed to drag my thoughts back to the present and to my life as it is now, and my spirits began to lift. I stopped, ate some food and told myself to get a grip.

In Four Crosses I met a man walking a Labrador puppy and I asked him for directions to the village shop. He told me, and asked me how far I was going. I explained about the Offa's Dyke Path.

He'd love to be able to do something like that, he said. He went on to detail a very high-flying career, cut short because of multiple blood clots caused by frequent flying, some of which were still inside him because doctors had been unable to remove them all.

We parted and I followed his directions to the shop, wondering as I did so whether he would ever have walked the Offa's Dyke Path if he had remained fully fit. I doubted it. From the international career trajectory he had described, if illness hadn't struck I think he would have just worked even harder.

All of which gave me much to think about, but I had things to do and I wasn't going to allow the skull cinema free rein again.

I bought three days' worth of food in the village shop, together with a packet of sandwiches for lunch, then took the whole lot up the road to a grassy verge where I stripped out all the unnecessary packaging, stowed what was left in my food bags, and ate lunch.

I re-joined the Montgomery Canal on the north side of Four Crosses and eased back into towpath walking once more.

Just after the aqueduct over the Afon Vyrnwy, the towpath turned a corner before a bridge and I found my way blocked by a family of swans. One adult stood by the waterside on the left, a group of cygnets spread themselves out across the towpath in front of me, and the other, smaller adult stood by the fence-line on the right. I assumed the larger swan near the water was the cob, or adult male, and the smaller one by the fence was the female.

I've found that birds and animals can react badly if surprised, so I try not to surprise them. I make some noise as I approach to let them know I'm coming, but not so much, I hope, as would alarm them. I also use my voice sometimes, keeping the tone calm and even.

So I slowed my pace but kept moving towards the swans, and as I did so I said, quietly, "Come on now, you can't have all the towpath, I need to come through here".

Neither the cygnets nor the cob seemed very interested in me and the idea occurred to me that I might get an easy passage. Then the female looked at me, looked back at her partner and hissed in that deliberately threatening way that swans have. But she didn't hiss at me – the hissing was firmly directed towards the cob by the water's edge. She couldn't have made it any plainer if she'd said it in English:

"Are you going to let him talk to me like that?"

The adult male turned wearily towards me, spread his wings and began to hiss. He had the air of a swan who was going through the motions. He knew I was no threat, but he also knew what was expected of him in the circumstances and Nature is a powerful driver.

The swans controlled the entire width of the towpath, which seemed to me to be more than they really needed. I knew that if I backed away they would be emboldened; I would still have to get past them, but the job would be made harder if they were to register an early success.

So I didn't back away, I ran at them. Specifically, I ran at the female, aiming to pass between her and the fence. I figured there was nothing to attack me on the fence side, so by taking that route one side of me was protected and any threat I faced would be all on one side, making it easier to defend against.

There was a blur of feathers and a lot of hissing and squawking, and I was through. I dodged through the gate and onto the road which crossed the bridge. The swans smoothed their ruffled feathers and I smoothed mine. Peace descended upon the towpath once more.

It was starting to rain, and I was rooting about in the pocket of my rucksack for my waterproof jacket when an elderly couple approached along the towpath from the opposite direction. We exchanged the usual pleasantries and I warned them about the swans, just out of sight behind the bridge. They thanked me and warned me about another lot just a little way in front of me.

Further up the canal I met a Belgian southbounder who, although his English was limited, also felt the need to warn me about the swans ahead of me.

This was getting too much. The anticipated confrontation was starting to mar the pleasure of what should have been an enjoyable part of the walk.

"Of course, these are not aggressive birds", he told me in

halting English.

My response, "They do a bloody good impression, then", didn't seem to translate and he went on his way. My reputation had evidently preceded me though, because the second family of swans failed to materialise.

The canal lead me gently into Llanymynech, where I knew I had some steep uphill to cover.

Llanymynech is unusual in that the England-Wales border runs down the centre of the main street. The families and businesses on one side have their refuse collection, policing, education, etc., provided by English authorities, while those directly opposite have their services provided by Welsh bodies.

In the recent past, when many Welsh counties did not allow the sale of alcohol on Sundays, anyone wanting to enjoy a drink on a Sunday had to cross to the English side of the village to do so. The border actually ran through the middle of one pub, meaning that, of its three bars, only the two which were in England could open on Sundays.

The rain had come to nothing so I took my jacket off in preparation for the steep climb ahead.

I was walking up to Llanymynech Hill, more exactly, up Llanymynech Rocks, a huge rock outcrop to the north of the village that was central to its *raison d'etre.*

Llanymynech Hill has been mined for at least 2,000 years. Bronze Age British people and Romans mined copper, lead and silver here, and from the early 1800s until the end of the First World War, Llanymynech Rocks was a productive limestone quarry. Limestone was taken out down inclined planes, either to local kilns or onward by canal (or, later, railway). Charles Darwin learned geology here in 1831, before embarking on HMS *Beagle* in December of the same year.

The English and Welsh limestone quarries at Llanymynech were rival enterprises until 1863, when the railway builder, Thomas Savin, took over both sides and ended years of bitter competition. Bankrupt in 1866 due to his railway schemes, Savin's creditors allowed him to keep the quarry and he threw himself into its management.

In 1867, Savin organised a massive explosion to increase the yield of stone, and in 1868 he went still further, with over four times the amount of explosive used in the 1867 big explosion. His plan was to extract a month's yield of rock in just one day, in front of an audience of assembled dignitaries.

At this point, I find that I pause and sigh.

Every book carries an implicit, unspoken contract between the author and the reader. An author works hard to create a rewarding emotional and intellectual experience and the reader, on his or her part, is honour-bound to give the resulting book a "fair go" before deciding whether to read it to the end or whether to chuck it unfinished behind the sofa, or to pass it off as new and give it to an unappreciated relative at Christmas.

An author aspires to entertain his customers, to engage with them, maybe to flirt now and then with the more attractive of them, sometimes to amuse them and at other times to arouse their better nature and higher instincts. On occasion he may even hope, whisper it quietly, to educate just a little. But whatever outcome he aims for, no writer wishes to be found predictable by his audience.

Unfortunately, this little piece of history contains over-ambition, a huge amount of explosive and very little in the way of health and safety legislation. I cannot alter history, my friend, I can only lay it out for your perusal. Dear reader, both you and I know that the next paragraph must begin with the words, "The resulting explosion..." and go on to catalogue devastation and destruction. We know it as surely as we know that night follows day. Literary convention will brook no less.

A deep breath, then. Are we ready? Let us join hands and take the plunge together.

The resulting explosion was heard ten miles away and debris fell over a mile from the site, damaging local houses and destroying the tramway bridge. Savin had to pay extensive compensation to householders whose properties were damaged. Perhaps it's best to give the last word to an eyewitness who, with classic British understatement, drily concluded his account of the explosion with:

"No other experiment of the kind has since taken place".

There has been no quarrying on the site for almost a century. Probably still using up the rock dislodged by Savin's great explosion, I thought. Whatever the reason, the result is a strange feeling of quietude, where the sounds of nature have once again resumed supremacy after being pushed out for so long by the noise of industry.

I left the quarries, pushed on uphill some more, and walked around the edge of the golf course which, naturally for this area, has fifteen holes in Wales and three in England. If you had a penchant for weak puns, you might say it's par for the course around here.

I could see only two men playing golf, which seemed

something of a waste given the time and effort it must take to maintain it all. I stood back from one of the greens and watched their approach shots, wondering what they thought of me, with rucksack and trekking poles. If they were regulars on this course they must be familiar with the sight of long-distance walkers. Did they ever wonder what it was like to walk the length of Wales? What a hiker sees and feels along the way? Did they ever think of doing the walk themselves? Or were we just part of the scenery, like something seen from a train window, noticed but quickly forgotten?

I walked back into the woods for a while, then steeply downhill again, across fields and into Porth-y-waen, my destination for the day. It took me some minutes to find Bankside, my campsite, but I was very glad I did. It was a lovely spot with everything I needed. The sun was out and although it was windy, I spent a comfortable night there.

I was woken in the early hours by strong winds and heavy rain. Hey, I told myself as I turned over and went back to sleep, that's what the tent's for.

But making an early start had become ingrained and I was up at sparrowfart once again. The weather had cleared and I sipped hot tea as I watched the day brighten while the wind dried my tent.

The morning was quiet and motionless as I walked along the lane from Porth-y-waen to Nantmawr.

I thought I'd aim for Froncysyllte and consider a night in bed and breakfast. Froncysyllte was only 24km away but staying there overnight would gift me the walk over the Pontcysyllte Aqueduct first thing the morning after. Quiet and understated, but remarkable in its vision and execution, the Pontcysyllte Aqueduct is one of my favourite places.

The hill behind Nantmawr was steep. The occasional wooded sections were cool and shady, but the treeless, unshaded stretches were hot.

In Trefonen, I stopped for a coffee outside the village shop. I didn't eat much because my appetite seems to drop in the first two weeks of a long walk, and then increase exponentially after that. I was still in the suppressed appetite stage, but I'd planned for around 3,000 calories per day, and I knew I was getting that. When I looked back on the walk afterwards, I realised that I need far more than 3,000 calories a day if I am to maintain my bodyweight on a long walk. It's hard to eat more when your appetite is dwindling, but I should have been shovelling down the food.

I passed the medieval ridge-and-furrow field system, still evident in the fields on the north side of Trefonen, then the line of houses which constitutes the hamlet of Tyn-y-coed. Then it was uphill once more, walking a broad footpath alongside the dyke. Dry, firm leaf-mould underfoot; overhead, mature broad-leaf and conifer trees. For my purposes, the day was an ideal one: moderate temperature, sun (but not too much of it) and a cooling breeze. I sat on a convenient bench and took on water.

Chapter 6

Skirting the Berwyns

Pretty soon I came to the edge of the trees, and a flat grassed area opened out in front of me, inclining gently upwards, with trees around its edges, and topped by the remains of a building.

I walked across the short grass to the stones.

A thousand feet up on a hilltop, I was at Oswestry Old Racecourse and what used to be the racecourse grandstand was right in front of me.

Horse racing first took place here in the 1600s. The wars with France supplied a labour force of captured soldiers and sailors, and these prisoners of war were deployed, perhaps "used" might be a better term, to lay new turf all around the course and to build the grandstand in 1804.

Race meetings lasted anything up to three days and a race entry cost two guineas, with a further half guinea to the clerk of the course[8]. There were often six races, with two or three

---

[8] *At that time Britain's currency, the pound, consisted of twenty shillings, each shilling comprising twelve pennies. A guinea was one pound and*

heats for each of them, and purses of between ten and thirty guineas were awarded to the race winners. Refreshment vendors paid one guinea, a sizeable amount in those days, for permission to operate on the course.

I stood in the ruined grandstand and tried to imagine the crowds and the horses but, try as I might, I couldn't evoke the feeling of past glories. While there are still signs of its former use, the site now looks like the common land it has become, and nothing like the social hub and entertainment centre it once was.

By the time of the 1840s, the racecourse on the hill above Oswestry was beginning to lose some of its social cachet. Outsiders and the lower orders were winning the prizes, rowdy behaviour caused people to stay away and attendances began to fall. This in turn reduced the gate money and the money which could be made from tradesmen and stall-holders.

As the national railway network developed in the middle of the nineteenth century, so the transport of horses around the country became easier. Unlike horses which had been walked to a racecourse, those carried by rail arrived fresh and ready to race, and the railways facilitated their carriage over longer distances, to bigger and more lucrative race meetings.

Eventually these factors became irresistible, and Oswestry Racecourse was abandoned in 1848.

But it would be wrong for us to abandon the old racecourse

---

one shilling (or £1.05 in modern money). Prices were often marked in guineas rather than pounds, right up to the decimalisation of the currency in 1971.

without mentioning one of its most colourful characters, a man obsessed with horses, who frequently attended race meetings here and who was known far and wide for his eccentricities: John Mytton.

Mytton was born in 1796, and inherited the family seat when his father died just two years later. John inherited wealth and a sizeable income, but signs of his eccentricity were never far away. He was expelled from prestigious Westminster School for fighting with a master. Sent to Harrow School, he was expelled again, this time after just a few terms. John's lack of academic excellence didn't prevent him from attending Cambridge University, but despite the 2,000 bottles of port he took to see him through, he found Cambridge boring and he never completed his studies.

The war with France had just ended as Mytton joined the 7th Hussars and he spent some time with the army of occupation there. At that point he must have appeared to be one of the most eligible men in the country: a cavalry officer, fantastically rich and from a good family. One can just imagine the ladies fluttering and swooning.

The Army lost its appeal and Mytton decided to stand for Parliament. He won his seat by handing out huge sums of money in ten pound notes to his electors, but as an MP he attended Parliament once, got bored after thirty minutes and gave up politics permanently. You can see the sort of thing the Chartists were up against a few years later.

Mytton kept forty horses and was so obsessed by them that he even named his son after one of his winners, "Euphrates". That number was reduced by one when Mytton made "Sportsman" drink a bottle of port and the animal died. Mytton himself was known to get through eight bottles of port a day, topped up with an indeterminate amount of brandy, but he also drank eau de cologne when nothing else was available.

In addition to his horses, Mytton kept 2,000 dogs, many of them dressed up in clothes and fed on steak and champagne, as well as sixty cats, also costumed and well-fed. He enjoyed dog fights, and bred and trained dogs for the purpose, even going so far as to fight them himself on occasion.

As a country gentleman of his time, it would have been odd if Mytton had not been interested in hunting and shooting. In fact, he loved both, although unlike his contemporaries, he sometimes hunted and shot while completely naked. On one occasion, when his hunt was disrupted by a coal miner who lived nearby, Mytton dismounted and went twenty rounds of bare-knuckle boxing with him before the man retired from the fight.

In 1826, for a bet, Mytton rode his horse into the Bedford Hotel in Leamington Spa, up the grand staircase and onto the balcony. From there, he jumped his steed over the startled diners below and straight through a window, landing in the street outside. Both horse and rider were unharmed.

Users of the English language in the nineteenth century had, perhaps, a certain robustness of expression which has been tempered in our modern-day society. People didn't mince their words, particularly where mental health was concerned, and John quickly became known as "Mad Jack".

Guests at a dinner party at Halston Hall near Oswestry were surprised when Mad Jack arrived dressed as a highwayman and riding a live bear. The "robber" rode the bear around the room, "holding up" the guests at pistol point. Everything went swimmingly until Mytton, desiring a touch more pace from his steed, applied the spurs, whereon the bear took umbrage and bit him in the calf.

By 1831, most of Mytton's property had been sold to pay his debts, but there were still large sums outstanding, so Mad Jack fled to Calais to avoid his creditors. On the way, he noticed an attractive 20-year-old woman named Susan on Westminster Bridge and offered her £500 a year to be his companion. She accepted, went with him to France and stayed with him until his death three years later in a debtors' prison in Southwark. Mad Jack was just 37.

Incredibly, although by then he was a pauper and well-past the height of his fame, 3,000 people attended John Mytton's funeral.

Interest in all things equine is still strong in the area, and just a mile or two further on is the Oswestry Equestrian Centre. A sign outside invited walkers to enter and use their facilities, so I did. Mad Jack would have damned their eyes and demanded a bottle of port, but I settled for a can of fizzy drink and recorded my thanks in the guest book.

I'd just closed the book when another walker came in. A southbounder, he had stayed in bed and breakfast at Froncysyllte last night and he recommended it to me. It seemed to tick all my boxes: reasonable price, agreeable owners and located right on the trail. I thanked him and jotted the details onto a leaflet inviting me to take riding lessons.

I passed the old lime kilns at Orseddwen and climbed Selattyn Hill where I was confronted by a group of women ambling towards me along a farm track. One of them seemed to be leading. She was carrying something white in her hand and she made a beeline for me, holding what I saw was a piece of paper in front of her.

"Do you know where we are?" she asked, in a strong Liverpool accent.

I could have opened my map and put my finger precisely upon my location, but I couldn't for the life of me find it on the poorly photocopied piece of paper she thrust in front of me. I played for time.

"I know where I am. I'm walking the Offa's Dyke Path. Where are you trying to get to?"

She named some place I'd never heard of, then, while I was still looking at her "map", she suddenly turned it through ninety degrees. I couldn't work out if she was trying to help me or trying to test me.

This wasn't the first time I've been asked by walkers for help with navigation. I always do my best to help, but it does strike me as odd that people are prepared to trust a random stranger with something so important. If I get my own navigation wrong, I've only myself to blame; but if I let someone else cock things up for me, well, I'd still only have myself to blame because the responsibility for knowing where I am and where I'm going rests with me and is not transferrable. So why other people try to transfer responsibility for their navigation onto my shoulders, I don't know.

I reached for my map to compare it with hers, as a quick way to help her find her location. There was a constant drone from behind her as the other women whiled away the time by chatting to each other.

"I can show you on my map," and I put my finger on it. "We're here, on Selattyn Hill."

"Never heard of it."

The tone of her voice indicated resolute disbelief and I almost felt compelled to justify my statement. Almost, but not quite. The woman looked at my map for about two seconds, obviously as bewildered by it as I'd been by her photocopy. Then, although she had nothing new to base it on, she appeared to make a decision.

"It's this way, girls", and she started striding the same way they'd been going when I first met them. She threw a "Cheers" at me over her shoulder as she went, as if I had somehow contributed to this new enlightenment, and the other women followed her, all still deep in conversation. I felt I'd been tested and found wanting, but I was glad they weren't walking the Offa's Dyke Path.

As I started my descent to Craignant, I could see the squat bulk of Chirk Castle looming on the far horizon ahead of me.

Chirk Castle was built by King Edward I to subdue the last princes in Wales and I was about to find out why they had to be subdued, at least from the perspective of successive English kings.

I was crossing the valley of the River Ceiriog and my path passed through the site of the Battle of Crogen.

King Henry II had taken large parts of Wales after his accession to the English throne in 1154. The Welsh princes saw their chance to regain the land and, in 1165, Henry gathered a large army to crush them.

Henry's plan was to march up the Ceiriog Valley to the Berwyn Mountains and to secure the castles there. The Welsh princes united to fight him and their ambush forces met the vanguard of Henry's army in the heavily wooded Ceiriog Valley.

The Welsh made the most of the dense woodland and ambushed from cover, so Henry ordered 2,000 woodcutters to fell trees and widen the passage for his army. The Welsh attacked at the point where Offa's Dyke crosses the valley and inflicted casualties before Henry's army were able to force their way through. One ancient tree, "The Great Oak of the Gate of the Dead", still stands on the site and is said to be the only living witness to the battle.

The information boards near the site present this engagement as a great Welsh victory. If it was, they probably wouldn't want too many victories of that sort: Henry's army was not repulsed, merely slowed down a little on its journey westwards.

Ultimately, Henry failed in the Berwyn Mountains. He took Welsh hostages and withdrew to Shrewsbury, where he oversaw the mutilation of 22 of them, including two sons of one of the Welsh leaders. The Welsh principalities survived for another 120 years, until they were overrun by Edward I, the originator of Chirk Castle.

I crossed the bridge over the River Ceiriog and started up the hill in front of me. I was taking the summer variant of the Offa's Dyke Path because it would route me closer to Chirk Castle and I enjoyed the shade provided by the estate trees as I followed the line of white-topped posts marking my way.

Chirk Castle was an abrupt return to civilisation, not because of any fault on the part of the castle, but because it is a tourist attraction and there were plenty of tourists there on such a lovely day. Kids shouted and squabbled, parents trailed after them, young couples walked under the trees with their arms around each other, lost in their own romantic worlds. Older couples, who had long ago said everything they had to say to each other, sat in silence over half-empty cups outside the coffee shop.

The small café didn't have much that was of use to me, so I bought a coffee and a bar of chocolate and took a table in the stables courtyard.

Chirk Castle stands on the hill to the north of the Ceiriog Valley, looking down on the site of the Battle of Crogen. It was completed by Edward I in 1310 and has been lived in for 700 years, for the last 400 by the same family.

The castle survived the Civil War, changing sides twice as a result of bribery rather than by force of arms, but it suffered extensive damage in 1659 at the hands of Parliamentarian troops and it was rebuilt after the Restoration in 1660. Today, it's a hugely imposing building.

When I'd finished my coffee and chocolate, I left Chirk and headed down a gently-sloping track into the valley of the River Dee. I thought back to the steep up and downs of The Switchbacks and counted myself lucky. I knew I had more hills to come, but that just made me appreciate the relatively level walk even more.

It couldn't last, of course, and it wasn't long before I was picking my way carefully down steep slopes again, across fields and stiles towards Froncysyllte.

I paused to chat with a southbound hiker, another man from Canada, and we discussed gear for a few minutes before tapping each other for information about the next stages of our respective walks. I learned that World's End and the Clwydian Range can both be tough cookies in bad weather, and the locations of a couple of campsites which I hadn't been aware of.

I headed across the field to the noisy A5 road and, just beyond it, the bed and breakfast that was my target for the day.

The A5 runs from Marble Arch in central London to Holyhead on the island of Anglesey, at the north-western tip of Wales. Holyhead is the country's main seaport for traffic travelling to Ireland.

The road as it is today is a product of the Act of Union, passed in 1800, which unified Great Britain and Ireland, and created the demand for better travel between the two places. An Act of Parliament in 1815 to facilitate this allowed the building of new roads and the compulsory purchase of existing turnpikes if necessary. The great engineer Thomas Telford was given the job of improving and constructing the road from London to Holyhead: the first state-funded non-military road building scheme in Britain since the Romans left in 410.

Telford, known punningly as The Colossus of Roads, started by improved existing turnpikes, but when he got to Wales he found himself building roads almost from scratch. The road was completed in 1826, and Telford regarded it as his greatest engineering achievement. Such was the quality of his work that the road is still the principal route through Wales to Holyhead and many of his original depots and tollhouses still survive.

Despite the warning signs and the fast traffic, the road was easy to cross, and there was my B&B. It was a weekend and I hadn't booked, but they still had room for me and I wallowed in the relative luxury of being indoors for a night. The next morning would see me cross one of Telford's earlier triumphs: the Pontcysyllte Aqueduct.

Chapter 7

Eglwyseg[9] and World's End

The next day dawned bright and clear, and I set out along the dyke as it traversed a field and lead me towards the canal. I was bright-eyed and bushy-tailed. I had enough food and clean clothes to last the rest of my trip, which only left me with water to worry about. The weather was fine and my pack felt light. Even the best-planned walk carries an element of uncertainty, but I was starting to get a feeling that my completion of this hike was no longer in doubt. All I had to do was walk 70km.

The canal ran horizontally along the side of the Dee valley and there were already boats moving on it as I crossed the bridge and stepped through the gate onto the canal towpath.

Originally constructed for the draught horses that pulled the canal barges, the towpath had recently been resurfaced and felt good underfoot.

When it was built, this canal was named the Ellesmere Canal and it was designed to create a transport link between the

---

[9] *16 points, in case you were wondering.*

mineral-rich hills of north-east Wales and the port of Liverpool. Branches were intended, to extend it to Llanymynech and to the River Severn at Shrewsbury, but rising costs prevented the canal from being completed as it had originally been planned. Like most canals, it struggled when the railways came, and closed just before the Second World War, but it has been re-opened in more recent years for leisure use.

What was, at the canal's inception, a water feeder-channel coming from Llangollen has also proved navigable for narrow-gauge boats. Nowadays, the canal is used solely for recreation and the former feeder-channel is promoted as the main boating route into Llangollen. The canal has been renamed the Llangollen Canal to reflect this.

The good weather seemed to have a contagious positive effect on everyone's morale and I was given cheery greetings by the boaters who passed me. Or maybe more than one mainbrace was being spliced early[10].

Across the valley ahead of me, the Pontcysyllte Aqueduct became visible through the trees lining the canal bank and I paused to take a look at it.

The aqueduct, the largest in Britain, carries the canal high above the River Dee. In essence, it comprises a series of "U" shaped iron troughs bolted together to carry the canal, supported on high stone piers above the river below.

The engineers responsible, Thomas Telford and William Jessop, knew that an aqueduct differs from a road bridge in one vital particular: Archimedes Constant dictates that as a

---

[10] *"Splice the mainbrace" is an order given on naval vessels, instructing that the crew be issued with alcoholic drink.*

boat crosses an aqueduct, the mass of the boat in the water displaces an almost equal mass of water from the aqueduct. This means that the vertical loading stresses on an aqueduct remain almost constant as traffic uses it, in contrast to a road bridge where the stresses imposed fluctuate as the traffic comes and goes.

That's not to imply that Jessop and Telford had an easy time of it. When they put forward their proposals, it was generally thought that their planned construction method would not work in practice, but Telford was confident after using the approach on a smaller scale elsewhere.

The project started in 1795 and took ten years to complete. The result stands 38m (126ft) above the river and is 307m (1,007ft) long, running straight across the Dee valley to the canal wharf at Trevor.

I carried on along the towpath, waving to more boaters as they cruised past me. Around a bend, enjoying the level walking, and then the trees opened out and there was the aqueduct, this time seen from the boaters' approach to it.

The aqueduct is every bit as splendid up close as it is from a distance. From afar, what strikes the observer most is its measured proportions and its impression of great solidity. Up close, what registers most is the drop. It's not often we get a chance to look down onto the tops of large trees and the effect is, at first, a little unsettling. And that drop brings home what a challenge it must have been to build it.

The edge of the iron trough carrying the canal water is just six inches above the water level, giving boaters the impression that they are sailing along the edge of a high cliff. Along the other edge there is a narrow footway for the draught horses that pulled the barges, guarded by an iron railing.

I started out along the footway, vaguely aware that in the far distance on the other side, someone was walking towards me. As I got nearer to the centre of the aqueduct that "someone" materialised into a coachload of Japanese tourists.

As I was more likely than them to be ungainly, because, unlike any of them, I was carrying a rucksack on my back, I hoped to take the railing side of the footway and let them step around me. But they were elderly and most of them were hanging on to the handrail, which would put me on the canal side of the footway with, if I toppled, nothing to catch me but the canal.

As they got closer, I saw that they weren't just hanging on to the handrail: they were gripping it for dear life, shuffling along, eyes fixed straight ahead, afraid that if they let go even for a split-second, gravity would exceed its bounds and swirl them over the edge and dash them onto the rocks in the River Dee below.

The only way to pass them, or to let them pass me, was for me to stand on the canal-side edge of the footway and turn sideways on, so that my heels and my pack projected behind me, over the canal water. This left just enough room for the coach party to hobble past, gripping the rail with at least one hand at all times, determinedly not looking down. There must have been about thirty of them, so it took a while for this cavalcade of terror to pass. I hoped their transport was going ahead, to meet them at the other side, or they'd have to do it all again to get back.

The March of the Damned eventually passed me by, and I had the towpath to myself once more.

When I stepped off the northern end of the aqueduct, I

looked back along it and marvelled. Not so much at the aqueduct, although that is remarkable, but at the thought that, even after building this sensation, Thomas Telford considered the A5 London to Holyhead road his greatest engineering achievement.

I was reminded, as I so often am when I'm walking, that a walking pace is a very effective way to take in my surroundings. Walking over the aqueduct showed it off well to me. I have driven on the A5 many times, aware of its history as I did so, but 60mph is not the best pace at which to absorb one's environment. Indeed, in that situation, the inside of the car becomes one's environment. Walking, on the other hand, is how human beings have approached settlements, and other humans, for millennia. We see and feel more when we approach a place on foot.

Was the aqueduct Telford's second greatest engineering achievement? I didn't know. I would probably have to walk the A5 to make a comparison, and people did walk long distances along it, in the days before the motor car. But you wouldn't want to walk it now, unless you had an unnatural fondness for traffic congestion, fumes and noise.

I turned and walked on to Trevor.

Once industrial, Trevor Basin is now devoted mostly to the maintenance and servicing of pleasure boats but, like the rest of the canal, it started out as an industrial site. The development of a chemical industry in the area in the 1860s ensured the canal stayed profitable for a further fifty years, because some of the chemicals were too dangerous to transport by road and the canal offered a safer alternative.

I climbed uphill, away from the canal, on a path that would take me halfway around Eglwyseg Mountain to World's End. I was glad of whatever shade I could get, but I was soon thrust out of the trees and onto the open hillside.

My way was along a road which followed the contours more or less, directly below the cliff and the scree slopes of Creigiau Eglwyseg. The good weather granted me sweeping views across the Vale of Llangollen and Castell Dinas Bran.

The little hill on which the castle sits looks the perfect site, and it must have looked almost a fairy-tale castle when it was in its prime. Sadly, all that remains today are ruins.

But the ruins you see at Castell Dinas Bran are not the first buildings on this site. That honour falls to a hillfort built at the start of the Iron Age. The remains currently visible date from the 1260s and were built following the Treaty of Montgomery in 1267, which recognised Llywelyn ap Gruffudd as Prince of Wales. The castle was fired in 1276 to prevent it falling intact into English hands. Castell Dinas Bran translates into English as "Castle of the city of the crows".

I kept on along the contour path. I'd met a few people, mostly kids on a school or D of E trip, but as I progressed up the valley it became quieter and more remote. I knew that just across the valley from me was Plas Ucha yn Eglwyseg, the home of John Jones Maesygarnedd, one of the regicides of King Charles I, but I couldn't make out which distant set of buildings it was.

After losing the Civil War, the king was tried and executed in 1649. When the monarchy was restored in 1660, Parliament passed the intriguingly named Indemnity and Oblivion Act, a general pardon for most crimes committed during the Civil War and the interregnum which followed. Unfortunately for Jones, the Act expressly omitted the regicides, that is, those who had put their names to the king's death warrant back in 1649.

John Jones Maesygarnedd made no attempt to flee and was quickly arrested and imprisoned in the Tower of London. He was tried and convicted, then taken to Charing Cross where he was hanged, drawn and quartered.

My path descended through a pine wood and I arrived at a ford where a clear, fast-flowing stream crossed the narrow tarmac road that would be my route for the next few kilometres. There was a bench by the stream, set back a little on a patch of grass amongst the pines, with a view of my route across the ford and up through the beech trees ahead. I decided it would make a good lunch stop.

Higher up the wooded valley to my right was the source of the stream in front of me. I was at World's End. I ate a chocolate bar and pondered what sort of people would call a place World's End, and why.

None the wiser after five minutes, I took off my shoes and socks, and aired my feet while I ate a cereal bar.

I was in no great rush to press on. I knew that the next couple of hundred metres were shaded, but my map showed me that the three kilometres after that were in the open sun. I sipped some water, then realised that sipping wouldn't do on a day like this and guzzled half the bottle.

Over the years, I've got a lot better at keeping myself hydrated while I'm walking. It seems a simple enough task: drink enough water. End of. However, my default method was to carry enough water, but not to drink much of it. That sounds like a contradiction and now, looking back, I can see that it is. But at the time my thinking was, if I drink this water, then I won't have enough. So I didn't drink it, I carried it. Often I would arrive at my destination with full water bottles and a smug sense of pride: I carried enough water, and look: here it is.

Maybe it's because I'm the product of a wet country, one in which water is never far away, a phenomenon that makes the idea of water-planning seem, well, unnecessary at best, strange at worst.

Over time, I've learned that a better approach is to plan ahead so that I know what water sources are available along the trail. That way I don't carry too much water (and I wouldn't want to because water is heavy). I also take care to fill myself with water before I leave a water source and to drink as I walk to the next one. Plan ahead, "camel up", don't carry to much water, drink what you're carrying. Common sense, really, but of course, despite its name, common sense is not always common.

I could have filled my water bottles in the clear mountain stream in front of me, but I knew I was only 6km from a village. A village which contained a pub, a shop and, if I got really desperate, houses I could knock on to ask for water. A mere 5km after that village was my intended destination for the day and that too had water. So I guzzled away happily, keeping only a small amount of water for the next 6km.

Satisfied that I'd lavished enough care and affection on my feet, I set off again, this time uphill along the tarmac road, under the shade of the beech trees, their bright green leaves reflecting the sunlight.

All too soon, I broke out of the tree cover and started across the open moorland. Both the weather and the terrain were similar to that I was expecting for the next day, so this served as an early taster of what was to come.

A bright, blue sky decorated with occasional puffs of white

cloud curved over me like a massive roof. Way, way below it, on the ground around me, the brown heather stretched for miles in every direction, patterned with green patches of new growth where it had been burned back to create food for grouse.

I paused and watched an adder wriggle across the dry, dusty path a pace ahead of me, passing from my left to my right and out of sight into the heather roots almost as quickly as the mental processes by which I realised what I was seeing.

I started on again, wondering what might have happened if I had been one pace further along the trail than I was when the adder crawled out.

Adder bites can be painful but they aren't usually fatal. The adder is the only venomous snake in the UK but, like many venomous snakes, it doesn't always inject venom when it bites. The National Health Service recommend that anyone bitten should stay in hospital for 24 hours for observation. Recovery takes one to two weeks for children and usually three weeks or more for adults. While an adder bite might not be dangerous, the NHS reckon that a quarter of adults bitten will take between one and nine months to make a full recovery. Only about a hundred adder bites are reported in the UK each year, with most bites occurring between June and August.

Had I been one step ahead of myself, I might have stepped on the snake, but adders are not aggressive creatures: it's more likely that mine would have waited until I'd passed before venturing out to cross the track.

I reached the edge of Llandegla Forest, the first section of which was the usual devastation that results from large-scale conifer felling. Once I'd crossed that and entered the woodland, I found that the forest itself was pleasant and shady. I'd read somewhere that it had recently been sold by its Finnish owners to the Church of England. Apparently that and other purchases have made the C of E the biggest private owner of forestry in the UK.

Although it's still a big landowner, the Church doesn't own as much land as it used to. In the nineteenth century it was the largest landowner in England. Most of that was farmland, usually rented out, but nowadays its land-holding is smaller in area and consists of more profitable commercial land. Most of the C of E's £5 billion portfolio is in stocks and shares, a fact that makes it difficult to avoid remembering the biblical exhortations to "sell all that thou hast, and distribute unto the poor".

Are there poor people in England? Not by international measures of poverty, like the World Bank's $1.25 per day income threshold. Worldwide, about 1.3 billion people are "poor" by the World Bank's definition, so if the Church of England were to liquidate all its assets, the poor around the world would receive less than £4 each.

I was distracted from this depressing train of thought by a sign of a type that I hadn't seen before. It featured a silhouette of a person carrying a backpack and walking with trekking poles, with a red diagonal line across him or her.

It clearly referred to me, indeed, it could have been me pictured on the sign. I read it as meaning "no walkers" and that puzzled me. Most places that want to keep walkers out put up signs reading "Private" or "No path" or something similar. I'd never seen one aimed so specifically at walkers before.

I scratched my head and tried to work it out.

Maybe it was the sun, or maybe the distance I'd walked, but

I must have been a bit slow that day and it took a practical demonstration before I understood.

There was a sound like someone violently rattling wire coat hangers in a big saucepan, quickly getting louder, and then a man on a mountain bike flashed across my path, with a friendly shout as he passed me.

I stepped back as another two mountain-bikers rattled and shook their way down the hill and I realised that some of the trails in Llandegla Forest were for walkers and some were for bikes, and never the twain shall meet.

Cycling and walking do seem to co-exist cheerfully in the forest and I noticed several more "no walkers" signs on side tracks, which served to keep me on the right path. I paused on a couple of occasions to give way to more mountain-bikers, but all too soon I was back out in the sunshine again, approaching the village of Llandegla.

Llandegla is located on what was once one of the main drovers' roads from Wales to England, that is, a route by which cattle were driven long distances to market. Many British towns and villages have a street named Longacre and the name derives from the drovers' habit of grazing their cattle along the verges of the drovers' roads. The verge was the "long acre". The advance of the railways in the nineteenth century provided a much more efficient way to move cattle and killed the centuries old tradition of droving in the UK.

I walked down the village's main street, teasing myself with the promise of an ice cream from the village shop when I passed it, only to come back down to earth with a bump when I realised that it was Sunday and the shop would, of course, be closed.

I nodded to a man washing his car, the only other person visible down the whole length of the main street.

At the north end of Llandegla the road forked around each side of the church. My route would take me to the right, past some cottages and the village's sewage plant.

I paused by the church. It was named St Tecla's, not a name I'd heard of before, and a sign outside invited me in for coffee.

I'm not one to look a gift horse in the mouth, however because of the ice cream fiasco, I was all too aware that it was Sunday, which meant the church would be holding services. I checked my watch to make sure my presence wouldn't be intrusive. Reassured that it wouldn't, I made my way inside.

The inside of St Tecla's fitted perfectly with its mid-Victorian exterior, although the site is probably much older. I made myself a coffee and took a couple of biscuits. Granted it was a village church in a quiet, isolated part of the country, but even so the sense of calmness and tranquillity was almost tangible. By the time I'd finished my coffee and biscuits I reckoned that ten minutes rest here was worth an hour's anywhere else.

I stepped outside, back into the lazy afternoon sunshine and some lines from Grey's "Elegy Written in a Country Churchyard" came into my head:

"The curfew tolls the knell of parting day,
The lowing herd wind slowly o'er the lea,
The ploughman homeward plods his weary way..."

I walked across the churchyard to the gate. The air was still and the village streets were deserted: quiet and empty in the sunshine. I pulled on my rucksack and resumed plodding my weary way.

Chapter 8

The Clwydian Range

Llandegla has another claim to fame.

A few miles south-west of the village is a farm called Plas yn Ial. Plas yn Ial was the family home of the Yale family ("Yale" is the anglicised version of "Ial").

In the late 1600s, Elihu Yale made his fortune in the East India Company, the private company which ruled the British colony of India on behalf of the British government up until the Mutiny in 1857.

In 1699, Yale returned to his family's roots and moved into a mansion near Wrexham. In 1718 he was asked for assistance by an educational establishment in New Haven, Connecticut, then, of course, also a British colony. Yale sent books, a portrait of the king and goods which were sold for a decent return. In gratitude, the establishment was renamed after him: Yale College, now Yale University.

I pressed on through the warm, drowsy sunshine. My intended destination for the day was Gweryd Lakes, at the south end of the Clwydian Hills, and I reached it with time in hand.

But while I might have had plenty of time to move on, I didn't feel as if I had the energy to match. It had been a long day and I wanted to save the Clwydian Hills so I could tackle them all in one day, which would be tomorrow. I pitched camp next to the lake, Llyn Gweryd.

Apart from a few anglers, I had the place to myself. I ate dinner seated on the short, dry grass, watching the swallows swooping for flies, lower down over the lake. I sipped my tea and considered what was left of my trip. A good day tomorrow should get me to Bodfari (22km away) or Rhuallt (30km). And if I could get to Bodfari or Rhuallt tomorrow, then an early start the following day would give me plenty of time to get to and explore my journey's end, the town of Prestatyn, and maybe get a train home into the bargain.

I felt elated that I was so close to completing my walk, but my excitement was tempered by the enforced finality which would be a component part of that completion. The destination was only important to me because it created the journey to reach it: it was the journey that mattered and the journey would be over.

I experience points on a long-distance walk, low points it must be said, when I tell myself that I'm never, ever going to do a long walk again. But I always do. There's something about the challenge, the environment and life on the trail that reaches out to me and finds a willing recipient reaching straight back.

I sighed and dug down once more into the packet of biscuits that I was slowly, but resolutely, demolishing. I lightened my mood by thinking about how completing the trail would reunite me with those I care about, and who care about me.

The sun was just beginning to dip beyond the hill to the back of me, its late rays clearly and brilliantly illuminating the trees on the other side of the lake before me. While I had been lost in my thoughts, the sun had slipped down and put my position into shade. No longer in the sun, I felt a slight coolness. I glanced around me: not a cloud in the sky, so probably a chilly night in the offing.

I flicked the dregs of my tea across the grass and began organising myself for the night.

Next morning, I was up just after first light. The sky was still clear and so the early-morning sun was slowly but surely warming everything, as it rose in the sky.

My tent was completely dry, both inside and out. I'd camped on grass, near water, through a chilly night, and with the tent tightly closed up, all factors which should have resulted in extensive condensation, but there was none, which was puzzling.

However, my focus was all on movement, so I didn't dwell on the condition of the tent: I simply stuffed it away, completed my personal admin and took breakfast.

It hadn't taken me long to eat and strike camp but by the time I got moving the sky had clouded over and a strong wind had sprung up, coming from the east. Mist was swirling around me as I left the lake and started back towards the trail.

I knew from the map that once I'd crossed the first three hills this morning, I would descend into a dip. A dip which contained a road and, more importantly, next to that road, a café.

A second breakfast would be most welcome, I felt. But I knew in my heart of hearts that I wouldn't get one. My success rate with pubs and cafes had been distinctly below par on this trip. The place would have been struck by lightning or wiped out by a meteorite by the time I got to it, of that I was sure.

I crossed Moel y Plas and Moel Llanfair. The cloud was low, but not low enough to prevent me from seeing miles into Wales on my left.

The Clwydian Range is a line of hills running north-south. I was starting at their southern end and walking along the whole range, a route cunningly contrived to include just about all the uphill and downhill that the Clwydians had to offer.

I crossed Moel Gyw ("moel" means "bald" in Welsh, and "bald" is a term still used in the USA to describe hills with no trees) and then started downhill again.

I could hear a faint hum of traffic noise and soon I could make out the road. Behind it was a set of buildings which, according to my map, must be the café. I couldn't see all of it, but what I could see looked unscathed by lightning or meteorite. I wondered what unseen devastation might cause it to be unable to serve me breakfast. Plague, perhaps?

I dropped down onto a track and passed a farm and some cottages, then emerged onto the side of the main road. Across from me was the café.

It was empty, locked up, with a large "For sale" sign decorating the vacant car park.

I wasn't surprised or disheartened: the situation had seemed inevitable. When you know you won't get breakfast, not getting it doesn't ripple your pond much. I had never doubted that the café would be closed – to my mind the only question to be resolved was the purely academic one, why?

And now I knew.

So it was with calmness and equanimity that I took off my rucksack in the café car park, stripped off my shirt and proved that men can multi-task, by eating a Snickers bar, checking my route on the map and applying sun cream, all at the same time.

After a decent interval, I wiped sun cream and chocolate off the map case and set off up the hill again. Moel Fenlli's hillfort dates from the Iron Age and the remains of 61 roundhouses, a dam and a freshwater stream have been found here. In 1816, after a heather burn, a cache of 1,500 Roman coins was found, suggesting a very long period of occupation on this site.

Another steep downhill and then I found myself tracking slowly uphill, in the direction of a squat, dark structure which seemed to lurk on the horizon to the north of me.

I was walking towards the Jubilee Tower on Moel Famau.

At 558m, Moel Famau is the highest hill in the Clwydian Range and it was this attribute that resulted in its being chosen as the site for the Jubilee Tower.

The tower was planned to commemorate the Golden Jubilee of King George III in 1810[11]. The foundation stone was laid that year but not much else happened because no design had been agreed.

Eventually funds were raised and work started in 1813. Egypt and things Egyptian were very fashionable at the time, so the tower was designed as an Egyptian obelisk. Three

---

[11] *The 50th anniversary of his accession to the throne.*

tiers were planned, with a 115ft obelisk sitting on top of a rectangular base, with four large corner bastions.

In 1815 work stopped due to a row between the builder and the architect, a hiatus which continued until 1817, when work resumed but on a lower tower.

By 1846, a combination of poor construction and bad weather were causing the tower to crumble, and it was still incomplete in 1862 when a fierce storm caused the obelisk to collapse. The remainder was demolished, leaving just the base, and most of the stone debris was removed and recycled.

The rectangular base, with its four corner bastions, can still be seen and the Egyptian style is still very much in evidence.

A bracing walk followed, along the crest of the hills, with the wind cooling the effect of the sun. I set a good pace where the path followed the contours, but there was plenty of uphill and downhill to liven things up. I walked under skylarks and over Iron Age settlements until I arrived at a steep little hill standing all on its own.

This was Moel Arthur. Moel Arthur was thought to be an Iron Age hillfort but Bronze Age and Roman artefacts have been found here, indicating that it was lived in for a long time before the Iron Age and a long time afterwards. The hill looks ideal for a defensible settlement: a small top, easily cleared of woodland, with steep sides which would make attack very difficult. The people at Moel Arthur would have lived inside the external rampart, in timber-framed roundhouses. From what we know of them, the roundhouses would have had a central hearth, and wattle and daub walls. Because wood rots, the only evidence that remains of these dwellings is a series of circular depressions in the ground, thought to be the result of rainwater dripping from the thatched rooves. Their Iron Age occupants were farmers, producing grain and meat, and gatherers who collected wild produce. Some of them were skilled metal-workers.

I suspected some sort of local legend linking the place to the ancient myths of King Arthur and the Knights of the Round Table but, other than the name, I haven't been able to find any connection.

There is evidence of ancient quarrying on Moel Arthur and gold was discovered in the area more recently, in 1888, unfortunately not in any great quantities.

Climbing up towards yet another Iron Age hillfort, this time Penycloddiau, I met my first Welsh Offa's Dyke Path hiker. She was walking southbound and despite the inconvenience of sunburned legs, a result she cheerfully admitted of her forgetting to apply sun cream, she was positive and bouncy, looking forward to her walk south.

I reached Penycloddiau, but didn't linger. I was pretty much saturated with Iron Age hillforts by that stage and I didn't have to dawdle to get the feel of the thing: at 21 hectares Penycloddiau hillfort is one of the largest in Wales, its ramparts and ditches sprawling all around me as I walked through it.

The good weather had helped me cross the Clwydians more quickly than I had expected, and I reached the end of the range and dropped down through forests and fields.

The air had been fresh and clean as I crossed the hills, and I wondered how it might compare with the air quality in central London. For all its other attractions, I didn't think London would come out of the comparison well.

But I needn't have devoted too much thought to the

comparison issue because, luckily for me, a man at the farm in the valley below was on the case. He'd piled up a bonfire of plastic containers and thrown an old mattress on top for good measure. The acrid smoke made me cough about a mile before I reached the smouldering pile of crap he'd painstakingly constructed. I thanked my lucky stars that I didn't live next door to him, or we'd end up on one of those reality TV shows, each talking about what a bastard the other was. Either that or the magistrates' court.

I passed to the windward side of the farm as quickly as I could and before I knew it, I was in Bodfari.

I checked my watch: only 3 o'clock. Last night's plan for today was well on track and I'd reach Rhuallt with a few hours to spare.

Looking to add a little extra food to my evening meal, I was disappointed to discover that the grocery shop in Bodfari had been transformed into an art gallery. I felt like pointing out to them that, while man might not be able to live on bread alone, he sure as hell can't live on pottery either. But then I noticed that the gallery had a small café on one side of it.

I was straight in and to my delight the gallery went on to redeem itself further: there was a small village shop behind the café. The ladies there sold me noodles and sliced ham, and then prepared a fantastic all-day breakfast for me.

Half an hour later, and much fortified by the all-day full English, I stepped out to complete the last seven kilometres to Rhuallt.

I quickly found that the café was well-placed and it was to the good that I'd stopped there. The next few miles were steep, so steep that when I stopped for the occasional breather, it seemed as if I could simply put my elbow out and lean on the trail in front of me.

I never fail to be surprised by the distance I can cover when I'm walking and I find it very satisfying to pause on a high point and to look back over the distance I've walked that day. Generally I find that, at best, I can see about half a day's worth of distance walked between where I'm standing and the far horizon. This afternoon I could see the moorland back above Llandegla Forest. It looked a very long way away, but I knew that it was only a matter of a few hours. That objective assessment of my hiking ability, combined with the knowledge that I'd reach Prestatyn early the next day, gave me a great lift.

The A55 road on the approach to Rhuallt came as a surprise and I paused at the start of the footbridge which crosses it, to take it in. Even though I'd been able to hear the main road from some distance away, and it had got slowly louder as I approached it, now that I was there it was an assault on the senses. Five lanes of moving metal glittered below me in the sunshine, flashing past in a continuous roar. I stood there for a full five minutes, for all the world like some stone-age Brazilian tribesman confronted with a city for the first time.

All of which showed me that it doesn't take long to slip into "trail-mode". It's a long way from "real" life and there's often something of a culture shock when you're suddenly brought back.

I crossed the bridge into the village of Rhuallt and the traffic noise faded behind me.

The village was quiet and I soon found the campsite I wanted to stay at. It turned out to be very upmarket, with expensive 4x4s towing new-looking caravans onto immaculately-gravelled pitches.

I wasn't sure how a dirty hiker would fit in with all this but I gave it a try and I was glad I did: the staff were polite and helpful and the washrooms were immaculate. I enjoyed a hot shower in a clean, roomy shower block with piped music, then I changed into clean clothes and headed for the bar I'd noticed when I checked in earlier. A few beers would really hit the spot, I felt, and if they served bar food, so much the better.

You're probably way ahead of me at this juncture, but I'll say it anyway for the sake of completeness: the bar opened six days a week but was closed on Mondays and, of course, it went without saying that today was Monday. Hey ho.

I trudged back across the tarmac car park to my tent on the grass. Although it was only about 100m, the walk from the closed bar to the tent was the hardest part of my day's walking.

I made myself a hot drink, more to fill the time than because I really wanted one, and took more time than usual to arrange my kit how I wanted it for the night. After that there wasn't much to do apart from getting an early night. I tried to tell myself that suited me, because I wanted to be up and away at first light, but I knew it wasn't true: I'd wanted a drink and some human company. As the poet said, into every life some rain must fall.

Next morning, I woke feeling refreshed and raring to go. The first rays of the sun were just starting to break over the trees and that was slowly causing a layer of early-morning mist to start rising.

I'd camped on grass, through a cool night with the tent tightly closed up. Similar conditions to those at Gweryd, but this morning the tent was dripping wet inside and out. Go figure.

The next six kilometres were soon under my belt and there I was, walking through the outskirts of my destination, Prestatyn. Up until that point Prestatyn had just been a name to me, but as I walked to its centre, it slowly unfolded and revealed its charms.

Prestatyn has few distinguishing features. It became a traditional seaside town with the advent of the railways in the nineteenth century and during the Second World War it was one of the few British towns to have been bombed by the Italian air force. In more modern times, it became the site of the UK's first major offshore wind farm.

Today, Prestatyn was thinking about going to work. I say "thinking" because there was some movement, but not much. The shops and offices had not yet opened as I walked down the main street. While I saw the usual signs of a struggling small-town high street, on the whole it seemed to be doing rather well.

I passed the railway station, noting its location for later use, and made my way to the seafront.

At first glance the seafront doesn't make too much of the fact that it's the finishing point of the Offa's Dyke Path (or the start, depending on your choice of direction). There's a boulder with a plaque on it, a twin of the one back on Sedbury Cliffs, and a finger signpost pointing to Chepstow.

But then you notice a large, shiny metal sculpture. This is *Dechrau a Diwedd,* a stylised representation of the sun.

Dechrau a Diwedd is Welsh for "beginning and end", a rather nice touch considering the seafront's dual role as far as the Offa's Dyke Path is concerned. A notice nearby explains how this works:

"Walkers starting their journey in Prestatyn will see the sculpture against the eastern sky, a metaphor for sunrise and the start of their journey.

Those who arrive into Prestatyn at the end of their trek will experience the sculpture in the western sky, a metaphor for sunset, the end of their journey."

I considered it a thoughtful way to celebrate the trail, and whoever commissioned and produced it seemed not only to grasp the duality of one location which is both start and finish, but also the fact that a long walk is very often the start or the end of something, and can even be life-changing. It seemed a fitting marker to end my journey.

It was time for breakfast, I decided.

I took a last look along the coast that I'd walked such a long way to see, and then turned away from it, wondering as I did so what my chances were of finding somewhere open for breakfast on this trip, and made my way back into Prestatyn.

Appendix A

Timeline

Confused by chronology? Disconcerted by dates?

Sometimes it's easier to place a date or an event if we can see the wider timeframe in which it sits. If your recollection of British history is a touch shaky, the chronology below might help you get things in the right order.

All the dates mentioned in this book are listed in chronological order, together with a few other significant dates for reference.

Date	Event
600BCE-50CE	The Iron Age. Many hilltops cleared of trees, hillforts constructed.
43CE	Roman invasion of Britain.
48-78	Roman conquest of Wales.
383	Romans leave Wales.

410	Romans leave rest of Britain.
500	Anglo-Saxon rule starts in England.
716-757	Aethelbald of Mercia builds Wats Dyke to protect his lands from the Welsh principality of Powys.
785-?	King Offa of Mercia builds Offa's Dyke between Mercia and the Welsh.
928	Athelstan, first King of England, sets the border between England and Wales.
1055	Gruffudd ap Llewelyn, King of Gwynedd, unites most of Wales under his rule and annexes parts of England.
1063	Gruffudd ap Llewelyn is defeated by King Harold of England and killed by his own men. Wales fragments again.
1066	The Norman Conquest of England. William the Conqueror establishes the Welsh Marches along the England-Wales border. Wales retains its own legal system, but the Marches are subject to neither Welsh nor English law and instead are ruled by their individual lords.
1066-1093	Sporadic warfare as the Normans conquer Wales.
1067	Chepstow Castle built.
1086	Domesday Book produced, detailing results of the Great Survey of England.

1094	A Welsh revolt against Norman rule wins back some territory.
1131	Tintern Abbey founded by the Cistercian order of monks.
1165	The Battle of Crogen. Henry II fails to crush the Welsh princes.
Late 1100s	The White Castle is fortified.
1200s	Monnow fortified bridge is built in Monmouth.
1216	King John destroys Kington Castle.
1216	Llywelyn the Great subdues all the other Welsh dynasties and becomes the preeminent prince in Wales.
1240	Llywelyn the Great dies.
1267	Under the Treaty of Montgomery, King Henry III of England recognises Llywelyn ap Gruffudd (known to the English as Llywelyn the Last), grandson of Llywelyn the Great, as Prince of Wales. This was the only occasion on which an English king recognised the legitimacy of a Welsh ruler.
1276	King Edward I invades Wales to remove Llywelyn the Last.
1277	The Treaty of Aberconwy makes peace but ensures the end of Welsh self-rule.

1282-3	Llywelyn's brother, Dafydd, is dissatisfied with Treaty of Aberconwy and rebels against Edward. Llywelyn is killed, Dafydd is captured and executed. Edward divides the Welsh principalities between himself and his supporters.
1284	The Statute of Rhuddlan formally "united and annexed" the principality of Wales to the Crown of England.
1310	Chirk Castle is built.
1350	St George supplants St Edward as patron saint of England.
1415	King Henry V defeats a numerically superior French army at Agincourt.
1485	Henry Tudor defeats King Richard III at the Battle of Bosworth Field and becomes King Henry VII. The Tudor dynasty is established.
1535	The "Laws in Wales Act" integrates Wales and the March into the English legal system. Monmouthshire is listed as a Welsh county. The Marches no longer exist.
1536	The Dissolution of the Monasteries by King Henry VIII. Tintern Abbey is stripped and closed.
1542	A further "Laws in Wales Act" does not include Monmouthshire in the list of Welsh counties.

Mid 1500s   White Castle abandoned.

1600s   Oswestry Racecourse is developed.

1642-1651   The English Civil War: Parliament versus the Crown.

1649   King Charles I is executed. One of the signatories of his death warrant is John Jones Maesygarnedd, brother-in-law of Oliver Cromwell and resident of Plas Ucha yn Eglwyseg near World's End.

1649-1660   England is a republic.

1660   The Restoration of the Monarchy. Act of Indemnity and Oblivion passed pardoning most crimes committed during the Interregnum. John Jones Maesygarnedd is tried and executed for his part in the death of Charles I.

1699   Having made his fortune in India, Elihu Yale returns to Wales.

1718   Elihu Yale sends goods to Connecticut, to be sold to provide funds for the Collegiate School. The school is renamed Yale College in his honour and later becomes Yale University.

1760   King George III crowned.

1793   War with France. Continues on and off until 1815.

1794   The Kymin roundhouse is built.

	Construction of the Montgomeryshire Canal starts.
1795	Work commences on Telford's Pontcysyllte Aqueduct on the Ellesmere Canal.
	Archibald Menzies brings the first monkey puzzle trees to Britain.
1796	John Mytton ("Mad Jack") is born.
1798	A British fleet under Nelson destroys the French fleet at the Battle of the Nile.
1800	The Kymin Naval Temple built.
	The Act of Union between Great Britain and Ireland creates demand for better communications between the two.
1804	French prisoners of war re-turf Oswestry racecourse and build the grandstand.
1805	Admiral Lord Nelson is killed at the Battle of Trafalgar.
	Telford's Pontcysyllte Aqueduct is completed.
1810	King George III's Golden Jubilee.
1811	The Welsh Methodist Church formally secedes from the Church of England. The WMC holds its services using the Welsh language, an important boost for the language as the education system in Wales

uses English, not Welsh.

1815	Napoleon defeated at the Battle of Waterloo. War with France ends.
	Construction of the London to Holyhead road (to reach Ireland) is started by Thomas Telford.
1821	John Davies protests his innocence but is hanged at Montgomery for robbery.
	The Montgomeryshire Canal is completed.
1826	The main London to Holyhead road is completed (now the "A5").
1831	Charles Darwin learns geology at Llanymynech and sets sail on HMS Beagle.
1834	John Mytton ("Mad Jack") dies.
1839	The People's Charter is published and the "Chartist" campaign for electoral reform starts. At a riot in Newport, 22 Chartists are killed by soldiers.
1840	Three of the Newport rioters are convicted of high treason in Monmouth, and sentenced to be hanged, drawn and quartered (the last time this sentence was passed in the UK). The sentences are commuted to transportation to Tasmania.
	The Post Office starts the penny post.
1848	Oswestry racecourse closes.

1857	The Indian Mutiny against British rule in India. The following year government by the East India Company ends and the British Crown begins direct colonial rule. India gained independence 90 years later.
1868	Thomas Savin's big explosion in Llanymynech quarry.
1902	Sir Arthur Conan Doyle publishes *The Hound of the Baskervilles* after staying near Kington.
1914-1918	The First World War. Construction of three "National Shipyards" near Chepstow with garden suburbs for shipyard workers.
	Llanymynech quarry closes.
1922	Solicitor Herbert Rowse Armstrong is hanged for murder.
1936	The Montgomeryshire Canal closes.
1939-1945	The Second World War (1941 - Deputy Fuhrer Rudolf Hess flies to Scotland to negotiate with Britain, detained, held for a time at Abergavenny, Wales).
1953	Queen Elizabeth II crowned. Memorial trees planted at Beacon Ring.
	Sir John Hunt (later Lord Hunt) leads first successful climb of Everest.
1967	Alan Ginsberg takes an acid trip at Tintern

Abbey and writes "Wales Visitation" as a result.

1971   The Offa's Dyke Path national trail is opened by Lord Hunt.

1972   The Local Government Act reorganises British counties and places Monmouthshire in Wales.

1974   Mike Oldfield releases the album "Hergest Ridge".

1998   The Government of Wales Act creates the Welsh Assembly to govern Wales. The Assembly gains law-making powers a few years later.

Part 2

Talking the Talk

A Spring Ramble

Chapter 9

Route Assessment

The Offa's Dyke Path is a marvellous walk, indeed, it has been listed by more than one authority as one of the world's greatest. The trail passes through three areas of outstanding natural beauty[12] and many areas of historical interest.

The route assessment in this chapter should provide enough information for you to work out, a) what time of year you'd like to hike the Offa's Dyke trail, and b) what you'll need in the way of clothing and equipment. It's up to you whether you walk it south-north, as I did, or north-south. Either way has the potential to be very enjoyable and there is no great advantage accruing to either direction.

The weather and climate information in the route assessment is for Knighton, which is mid-way on the walk. Bear in mind, though, that Knighton is only about 200m above sea level: the weather frequently varies with height and can be more extreme in the hills.

---

[12] *The Wye Valley, the Shropshire Hills and the Clwydian Hills.*

Route Assessment – Offa's Dyke Path

Distance / Height

Distance: 272km (170mi).
Ascent: 9,058m (29,718ft).
Highest point: Pen y Beacon, 706m (2,316ft).
Lowest point: Sea level (Chepstow and Prestatyn).

Climate and Weather

January

Temperature, average high: 6C / 43F
Temperature average low: 2C / 36F
Temperature, record high: 12C / 54F
Temperature record low: -9C / 16F
Precipitation: 51mm
Type / frequency (days):   rain 20, snow 4
Humidity: 86%
Wind average: 15km/h / 9mph
Wind record: 69km/h / 43mph
Sunshine: 4hrs/day
Sunrise / sunset: 0814 / 1628
Daylight: 8h 14m

February

Temperature, average high: 7C / 44F
Temperature, average low: 2C / 36F
Temperature, record high: 16C / 61F
Temperature, record low: -10C / 14F
Precipitation: 43mm
Type / frequency (days):   rain 19, snow 5

Humidity:	83%
Wind average:	17km/h / 11mph
Wind record:	96km/h / 60mph
Sunshine:	4hrs/day
Sunrise / sunset:	0727 / 1725
Daylight:	9h 58m

March

Temperature, average high:	9C / 48F
Temperature average low:	4C / 39F
Temperature, record high:	19C / 66F
Temperature record low:	-6C / 22F
Precipitation:	41mm
Type / frequency (days):	rain 20, snow 3
Humidity:	79%
Wind average:	17km/h / 10mph
Wind record:	70km/h / 44mph
Sunshine:	6 hrs/day
Sunrise / sunset:	0625 / 1816
Daylight:	11h 50m

April

Temperature, average high:	11C / 52F
Temperature average low:	4C / 39F
Temperature, record high:	21C / 70F
Temperature record low:	-4C / 25F
Precipitation:	52mm
Type / frequency (days):	rain 18, snow 2
Humidity:	75%
Wind average:	14km/h / 8mph
Wind record:	56km/h / 35mph
Sunshine:	8 hrs/day
Sunrise / sunset:	0613 / 2010
Daylight:	13h 56m

May

Temperature, average high:	15C / 58F
Temperature average low:	7C / 45F
Temperature, record high:	26C / 78F
Temperature record low:	-1C / 31F
Precipitation:	57mm
Type / frequency (days):	rain 20
Humidity:	74%
Wind average:	12km/h / 7mph
Wind record:	46km/h / 29mph
Sunshine:	8hrs/day
Sunrise / sunset:	0516 / 2101
Daylight:	15h 44m

June

Temperature, average high:	18C / 64F
Temperature average low:	10C / 50F
Temperature, record high:	31C / 87F
Temperature record low:	2C / 35F
Precipitation:	53mm
Type / frequency (days):	rain 19
Humidity:	74%
Wind average:	12km/h / 8mph
Wind record:	56km/h / 35mph
Sunshine:	9hrs/day
Sunrise / sunset:	0449 / 2136
Daylight:	16h 46m

July

Temperature, average high:	20C / 69F
Temperature average low:	12C / 54F
Temperature, record high:	30C / 86F
Temperature record low:	6C / 43F
Precipitation:	55mm

Type / frequency (days):	rain 19
Humidity:	74%
Wind average:	12km/h / 7mph
Wind record:	46km/h / 29mph
Sunshine:	7hrs/day
Sunrise / sunset:	0508 / 2127
Daylight:	16h 18m

August

Temperature, average high:	20C / 67F
Temperature average low:	11C / 52F
Temperature, record high:	33C / 91F
Temperature record low:	4C / 38F
Precipitation:	59mm
Type / frequency (days):	rain 21
Humidity:	76%
Wind average:	11km/h / 7mph
Wind record:	63km/h / 39mph
Sunshine:	6hrs/day
Sunrise / sunset:	0555 / 2037
Daylight:	14h 41m

September

Temperature, average high:	16C / 61F
Temperature average low:	9C / 47F
Temperature, record high:	25C / 77F
Temperature record low:	0C / 32F
Precipitation:	59mm
Type / frequency (days):	rain 21
Humidity:	81%
Wind average:	11km/h / 7mph
Wind record:	56km/h / 35mph
Sunshine:	6hrs/day
Sunrise / sunset:	0646 / 1927
Daylight:	12h 40m

October

Temperature, average high:	12C / 54F
Temperature average low:	7C / 45F
Temperature, record high:	23C / 74F
Temperature record low:	-3C / 27F
Precipitation:	70mm
Type / frequency (days):	rain 24
Humidity:	84%
Wind average:	11km/h / 7mph
Wind record:	65km/h / 40mph
Sunshine:	5hrs/day
Sunrise / sunset:	0737 / 1817
Daylight:	10h 40m

November

Temperature, average high:	8C / 47F
Temperature average low:	4C / 39F
Temperature, record high:	16C / 60F
Temperature record low:	-7C / 19F
Precipitation:	58mm
Type / frequency (days):	rain 20, snow 1
Humidity:	88%
Wind average:	11km/h / 7mph
Wind record:	61km/h / 38mph
Sunshine:	3hrs/day
Sunrise / sunset:	0733 / 1619
Daylight:	8h 46m

December

Temperature, average high:	6C / 42F
Temperature average low:	2C / 36F
Temperature, record high:	13C / 56F
Temperature record low:	-10C / 15F
Precipitation:	64mm

Type / frequency (days):   rain 20, snow 4
Humidity: 87%
Wind average: 13km/h / 8mph
Wind record: 69km/h / 43mph
Sunshine: 4hrs/day
Sunrise / sunset: 0815 / 1559
Daylight: 7h 43m

Terrain

Footpaths and farm tracks, through farmland, valleys, over hills, bogs and moorland. Uneven ground, steep slopes. Often wet.

Vegetation

Farmland on lower ground, open moorland on higher ground. The farmland is mainly dairy and sheep-grazed fields and hills. There is little forest cover.

Vegetation density is low.

The main allergens are pollens. Their peak release periods are:

> Grass pollen: June and July.
> Tree pollen: mid-February to mid-July.
> Weed pollen: May to mid-August.

Navigational Aids

The route is mostly very open with visibility occasionally restricted by weather, but not by vegetation or terrain.

The topography is not difficult to navigate across and can be used to assist navigation from:

> Sedbury to Monmouth (riverside walk),
> Pandy to Hay (ridge walk) and,
> Gladestry to Kington (ridge walk).

The trail is of good quality and follows existing tracks, footpaths and bridleways. It is well marked throughout its length by acorn signs and arrow signs (see back cover).

Sun Exposure

The altitude of the Offa's Dyke Path varies from sea level to 706m. In terms of protection from the sun, tree cover is largely insignificant.

Availability of Water and Food

Water is readily available from campsites, pubs, bed and breakfast establishments, public conveniences, shops (bottled water) and from farms or streams (avoid streams in areas grazed by livestock and treat stream water before drinking). A number of water points, provided specifically for walkers on this trail, are listed in the data sheet.

Food is plentiful, whether from pubs, cafes and restaurants, or unprepared from shops. The data sheet shows the main sources of food.

Problematic Wildlife

There are only minimal wildlife hazards on this walk. Farm dogs can occasionally cause problems and tick bites carry a risk of Lyme Disease. The likelihood of either is very low.

Remoteness

The remoter stretches of this path, i.e. those not close to a town, are from:

> Pandy to Hay (a 23km (14.3mi) stretch in the Black Mountains) and,

> Llandegla to Bodfari (a 28km (17.4mi) stretch along the Clwydian Range.

In the event of an emergency, possible barriers to self-rescue are steep slopes, bogs, rough terrain and poor mobile telephone reception. Leaving the trail at a point other than Chepstow or Prestatyn will usually involve a taxi ride to somewhere with a railway station.

Natural Hazards

Heavy rain (risk of wet clothing, wet kit, and exposure).

Fog (can adversely affect navigation).

Steep uphill and downhill slopes between Knighton and Brompton crossroads.

Combinations of the above.

Chapter 10

Logistics

What to Take

Your choice of equipment will be determined mostly by the information in the route assessment for the month in which you have decided to walk, and by whether you intend to camp or make your overnight stops in pubs, hostels, B&Bs, etc.

At any time of year you will need trail shoes or boots, rain gear (usually a jacket and over-trousers) and sun protection would be a prudent choice in spring, summer and autumn. Trekking poles will be very useful over almost all of this walk: if you've never used them, this is the ideal time to give them a try!

The usual caveats apply: wear footwear that doesn't give you blisters and avoid cotton clothing (it absorbs moisture and chills the wearer when wet).

How to Get There

The towns at each end of the Offa's Dyke Path, Chepstow

and Prestatyn, are both on the national rail network. If you'd like a cheaper alternative than rail travel, both are also served by National Express coaches.

Accommodation

The Offa's Dyke Path offers extensive opportunity for "wild camping".

Wild camping, i.e. camping other than on a campsite, is not illegal in England and Wales, but you are obliged to leave if you're asked to do so by a landowner or his agent. I've never had a problem with wild camping, and I advocate a scrupulous code for campers:

1. Take nothing, leave nothing. In particular, leave no trace. No litter, no fireplace, nothing.

2. Be as unobtrusive as possible. Pitch out of sight of the path and any nearby houses, don't light fires, use a drab coloured tent. Pitch camp as late as is practicable, strike camp as early as you can.

3. Treat landowners with respect and courtesy whenever you meet them. If it's practicable, ask permission to camp.

There are a selection of campsites along the northern two thirds of the path, but not much in the first 60-70km north of Chepstow.

If camping's not your thing, there is plentiful "in-brick" accommodation along the whole trail. You'll have a choice of pubs and inns, hotels, bed and breakfasts, bunkhouses and hostels, and many B&Bs will drive you to and from the trail if asked. A full and up-to-date list of accommodation, of all types and classes (including campsites) is maintained by the Offa's Dyke Association and available for free on their website (see Appendix B – Useful Websites).

Navigation

The Offa's Dyke Path is a national trail and so is well-marked and signed.

Parts of it are signed up with a circular sign containing an arrow and the words "Offa's Dyke Path" in English and in Welsh. Other footpaths are marked with similar signs but without the "Offa's Dyke Path" legend, so check carefully to ensure you're not diverting yourself away from the Offa's Dyke Path and onto a regular footpath by mistake!

Harvey produce two excellent maps which together cover the whole trail at a scale of 1:40,000. They are a good way to keep the weight you're carrying to a minimum and they're waterproof, so you can dispense with a map case.

If you prefer a map showing more of the countryside through which you're walking than a strip map can, you have a choice.

Ordnance Survey show the trail on eight 1:50,000 maps. Look for OS Landranger map numbers 116, 117, 126, 137, 148, 161, 162 and 172.

If you crave still more detail, Ordnance Survey also produce 1:25,000 maps, but you'll need a whopping ten of these: OS Explorer map numbers 13, 14, 167, 201, 216, 240, 255, 256, 264 and 265.

The OS maps have the advantage that you can see a large area around your location, allowing you to better appreciate, for instance, why castles are located where they are. The Harvey maps offer a significant weight-saving. The quality of both is excellent.

I'd also advocate a compass. I only used mine a few times, but I was glad of it when I needed it.

Chapter 11

Data Sheet

In this chapter, the route of the Offa's Dyke Path is described from south to north. When walking, find your location on the path and then refer to the data sheet. By that method you will be able to plan ahead in order to re-provision, visit interesting sites, camp, etc.

For each location, distance is shown (in bold) from the last location and cumulatively, in both kilometres and miles. The location name is shown in italics, followed by its facilities, then places of interest, thus:

Km from last (cum km) / Miles from last (cum miles)
Place name
Facilities.
Places of interest.

Indented entries are off the trail.

Shops, pubs, etc., sometimes change their opening hours and services, so if you intend to depend heavily upon one or more facilities, check before you leave!

0km (0km cumulative) / 0mi (0mi cumulative)
Chepstow
Post office, ATM, shops, cafes, pubs, railway station.
Chepstow Castle.

3.6km (3.6km) / 2.2mi (2.2mi)
Sedbury Cliffs
Start of the Offa's Dyke Path.

1.2km (4.8km) / 0.7mi (2.9mi)
Sedbury
Post office, shop, pub.
View of Chepstow Castle across the river.

2.8km (7.6km) / 1.7mi (4.6mi)
Woodcroft
Wintour's Leap. Tintern Abbey over river 5km on from
Woodcroft.

7.8km (15.4km) / 4.9mi (9.5mi)
Path splits into two. Choose from a high and a low option.
Paths re-join in 6km (3.8mi).

6.0km (21.4km) / 3.8mi (13.2mi)
High and low paths merge.

5.6km (27km) / 3.6mi (16.8mi)
Lower Redbrook
Pub.

2.8km (29.8km) / 1.7mi (18.5mi)
The Kymin
Naval Temple and Roundhouse.

2.8km (32.6km) / 1.7mi (20.2mi)
Monmouth
Shops, post office, pubs, cafes, restaurants, ATMs, WC, camping: Monmouth Caravan Park (Rockfield Road – 01600 711745), Monnow Bridge Caravan Site (Drybridge Street – 01600 714004).
Monmouth Castle, Monnow Bridge.

5.0km (37.6km) / 3.2mi (23.4mi)
Hendre
Camping: Hendre Farmhouse Orchard Campsite (01600 740484, 07973 814774). Bunkhouse: Rickyard Bunkhouse (The Rickyard – 01600 740128).

7.6km (45.2km) / 4.7mi (28.1mi)
Llantilio Crossenny

3.2km (48.4km) / 2.0mi (30.1mi)
White Castle
The White Castle (closed Mon, Tue).

4.6km (53.0km) / 2.8mi (32.9mi)
Llangattock Lingoed
The Hunter's Moon Inn (food, rooms, 01873 821499).

3.6km (56.6km) / 2.3mi (35.2mi)
Pandy / Llanvihangel Crucorney
Pandy:
Camping: The Rising Sun pub (also rooms, food, bar, wifi, 01873 890254), just south of the path. Bunkhouse: The Old Pandy Inn (also food, 01873 890208), at north end of Pandy.
Llanvihangel Crucorney:
Shop, camping: Pen Y Dre Farm (01873 890246).

8km (64.6km) / 5.0mi (40.2mi)
Longtown (3km (1.9mi) east of route)
Pub, post office, shop, camping: Tan House
Farm (01873 860221 / 860444, breakfast,
snacks).

8km (64.6km) / 5.0mi (40.2mi)
Llanthony (3km (1.9mi) west of route)
Pub, camping (Court Farm, cold water only,
01873 890359).

10.6km (75.2km) / 6.5mi (46.7mi)
Capel y Ffin (1.4km (0.9) off route)
Camping (The Grange, NP7 7NP, 01873
890215, breakfast, snacks, dinner).

17.6km (74.2km) / 10.9mi (46.1mi)
Hay Bluff

5.4km (79.6km) / 3.4mi (49.5mi)
Hay-on-Wye
ATM, post office, shops, cafés, pubs, camping: Radnors
End, HR3 5RS (01497 820780, near Boatside Farm).

(79.6km) / (49.5mi)
Clyro (2km off route)
Camping and bunkhouse (Baskerville Hall
Hotel, Clyro Court, HR3 5LE, breakfast and
dinner).

2.8km (82.4km) / 1.7mi (51.2mi)
Bronydd
Camping: Black Mountain View Caravan Park, (Bushfield
Farm, HR3 5RX - book in advance).

9.6km (92.0km) / 6.0mi (57.2mi)
Hill House
Water point.

3.0km (95.0km) / 1.8mi (59.0mi)
Gladestry
Pub, campsite (The Royal Oak Inn, rooms, tents allowed in garden). Hergest Ridge ahead.

2.9km (97.9km) / 1.8mi (60.8mi)
Kington
ATM, café, shop, WC, pubs, post office, Youth Hostel (The Old Hospital, Victoria Road, HR5 3BX, 01544 232745, 0870 770 6128), camping: Fleece Meadow Caravan and Camping Site (Mill Street, 01544 231235).

13.1km (111.0km) / 8.1mi (68.9mi)
Dolley Green
Water point at rear of Baptist church.

7.7km (118.7km) / 4.8mi (73.7mi)
Knighton
Pubs, cafés, ATM, post office, WCs.
Offa's Dyke Centre.

1.0km (119.7km) / 0.6mi (74.3mi)
Panpunton
Campsite (just over railway bridge, LD7 1TN).

4.6km (124.3km) / 2.9mi (77.2mi)
Carbett Hall
Water point.

4.4km (128.7km) / 2.7mi (79.9mi)
Springhill Farm
Camping and rooms (also meals, 01588 640337).

2.0km (130.7km) / 1.3mi (81.2mi)
Newcastle
The Crown Inn (food, rooms, 01588 640271, 07981 194287).

1.6km (132.3km) / 1.0mi (82.2mi)
Bryndrinog
Water point, B&B.

10.4km (142.7) / 6.5mi (88.7mi)
Mellington Hall
Caravan Park (with camping, bar and café, 01588 620011).

2.8km (145.5km) / 1.7mi (90.4mi)
Little Brompton Farm
B&B.

4.0km (149.5km) / 2.5mi (92.9mi)
Montgomery
Post office, ATM, pubs, shop.
Castle, hillfort.

1.6km (151.1km) / 1.0mi (93.9mi)
Forden
Camping and bunkhouse (Meadow Rise, Cwn Lane, SY21 8NB, 01938 580243).

4.8km (155.9km) / 3.0mi (96.9mi)
Kingswood
B&B (Heath Cottage Farm, Mary Payne, 01938 580453), pub (The Cock Hotel, food).

9.2km (165.1km) / 5.7mi (102.6mi)
Buttington
Pub and camping (The Green Dragon Inn, 01938 553076).

165.1km / 102.6mi
Welshpool (2km (1.2mi) off route)
ATM, post office, shops, café, pubs.

3.2km (168.3km) / 2.0mi (104.6mi)
Pool Quay
Pub.

168.3km / 104.6mi
Ardleen (2.4km (1.5mi) off route)
Pub (The Horseshoe Inn, food, rooms, 01938 590690).

8.8km (177.1km) / 5.4mi (110.0mi)
Four Crosses
Shop, post office, pubs, camping: The Golden Lion (also food and B&B, 01691 830295);

4.4km (181.5km) / 2.7mi (112.7mi)
Llanymynech
Post office, shop, café, pub.

181.5km / 112.7mi
Pant (1.5km (0.9mi) off route)
Pub (Cross Guns Inn, food), café.

3.6km (185.1km) / 2.3mi (115.0mi)
Porth-y-waen
Camping: Bankside (Blodwell Bank, SY10 9HP, also breakfast (book breakfast in advance), 01691 829169).

185.1km / 115.0mi
Treflach (1.5km (0.9mi) off route)
Pub (The Royal Oak Inn, food).

5.2km (190.3km) / 3.2mi (118.2mi)
Trefonen
Pub (The Barley Mow, food), post office, shop, café (in shop).

> 190.3km / 118.2mi
> *Oswestry* (3km off route)
> ATM, post office, shops, cafes, pubs.

8.8km (199.1km) / 5.5mi (123.7mi)
Craignant

4.0km (203.1km) / 2.5mi (126.2mi)
Chirk Castle
WC, café.
Castle.

5.6km (208.7km) / 3.5mi (129.7mi)
Froncysyllte
Post office, WC, café.
Pontcysyllte Aqueduct, Telford's A5 road.

1.2km (209.9km) / 0.7mi (130.4mi)
Trevor
Pubs.

> 209.9km / 130.4mi
> *Cefn Mawr* (2.8km (1.7mi) off route)
> ATM, post office, pubs, café, shops.

> 209.9km / 130.4mi
> *Bryn Howel* (2.8km (1.7mi) off route)
> Bryn Howel Hotel, bar food, no camping.

16.0km (225.9km) / 10.0mi (140.4mi)
Pen-y-stryt
Pub (Crown Hotel, food).

0.4km (226.3km) / 0.2mi (140.6mi)
Llandegla
Post office, shop.

4.8km (231.1km) / 3.0mi (143.6mi)
Gweryd Lakes
Camping.

4.4km (235.5km) / 2.7mi (146.3mi)
Clwyd Gate
Café (closed)

3.6km (239.1km) / 2.2mi (148.5mi)
Moel Fenlli
Hillfort.

3.2km (242.3km) / 2.0mi (150.5mi)
Moel Famau
Jubilee Tower.

4.4km (246.7km) / 2.8mi (153.3mi)
Moel Arthur
Hillfort.

2.8km (249.5km) / 1.7mi (155.0mi)
Penycloddiau
Hillfort.

4.8km (254.3km) / 3.0mi (158.0mi)
Bodfari
Pub (Downing Arms, food), café and shop in art gallery, camping: Station House Caravan Park.

6.8km (261.1km) / 4.2mi (162.2mi)
Rhuallt
Camping: The White Horse caravan site (with bar).

261.1km / 162.2mi
Dyserth (1.6km (1mi) off route)
Pubs, post office, WC, shop.

261.1km / 162.2mi
Meliden (0.8km (0.5mi) off route)
Post office, shop, pub, camping.

10.8km (271.9km) / 6.8mi (169.0mi)
Prestatyn
ATM, post office, shops, cafes, pubs, railway station, camping: Nant Mill Farm (Gronant Rd, LL19 9LY) also Lyons St Marys (Mostyn Rd, LL19 9TB, 2km east of Nant Mill, on A548).

A Spring Ramble

Appendix B

Useful Websites

The Offa's Dyke Association

The ODA is an independent voluntary organisation that promotes and protects the Offa's Dyke Path. Their website has extensive information about the path, accommodation and, of course, the dyke. They also sell maps and guides.

www.offasdyke.demon.co.uk

National Trails

National Trails are long-distance footpaths and bridleways in England and Wales. National Trails are administered by Natural England (an agency of the UK government) and National Resources Wales (a body sponsored by the Welsh government). Their website carries much information about all the national trails and material which will help you plan your hike along the Offa's Dyke Path.

www.nationaltrail.co.uk

Index

D

E

Restoration of the Monarchy, (1660), 92, 123
Rhuallt, 108, 114, 115
Robber's Grave, The Legend of. *See* Davies, John.
Route Assessment, 131-139
Royal Monmouthshire Royal Engineers (Militia), 27

S

Savin, Thomas, 80-81, 126
Scrabble, 39
Sedbury Cliffs, 12, 13, 5, 16, 117
Selattyn Hill, 88-89
Severn, River, 12, 16, 71, 73-74, 75, 95
Severn Valley, 68
Shropshire Hills, 54
Snake bites, 102
Springhill Farm, 58-61
St Cadoc's Church, (Llangattock Lingoed), 34
St Tecla's Church, (Llandegla), 105
Sunrise/sunset times. *See* Route Assessment.
Swan menace, 77-79
Switchbacks, The, 57, 61, 62

T

Telford, Thomas, 93, 95-98, 124, 125
Tennyson, Alfred Lord, 22
Terrain, 137
Timeline, 119-127
Tintern Abbey, 21, 22, 121, 122, 126
Transport, 140-141
Trefonen, 83
Trevor, 96, 98
Tudor, Henry. *See* Henry VII, King.
Turner, JMW, 22

Other books by John Davison

Every Day Above a New Horizon

In 1878 Robert Louis Stevenson, the author of Treasure Island and Kidnapped, walked across the south of France with a donkey. His plan was to write an account of his journey and to use the proceeds to fund a trip across the Atlantic to re-join the love of his life in the USA.

Inspired by Stevenson's account, John Davison finds himself constrained by his job in London and by his family commitments. Far from making things better, a series of short hiking trips in the UK only serve to fan the flame until, finally, the opportunity presents itself.

John sets off in Stevenson's footsteps, sensibly without the donkey, through blazing sun and driving rain, across one of the least populated parts of Europe; encountering kind, generous people, leavened with the occasional idiot, meeting them all with an keen eye and a dry sense of humour as he heads towards journey's end: the golden city down on the plain.

This is the art of the possible: John tells the story of one man's journey with just enough "how-to" to inspire you to start your own…

If you are old enough, you'll remember the Apollo space missions taking off from Cape Kennedy. And you might remember the countdown, 10, 9, 8 and so on, right down to zero! At that point, right when you might have expected the rocket to soar up into the sky, nothing happened. Well, nothing obvious happened. In reality, of course, there was lots going on. All systems were go, the engines had fired and were now building up power to thrust the huge rocket into space. At zero! there wasn't much to see, but we all knew that something momentous was about to happen.

So it was in the back bar of the Ardlui Hotel. There wasn't anything obvious to see, but everyone knew that something was going to happen...

Reviewers say:

"A truly inspiring read, written from the heart of a man with enthusiasm and passion for walking."

"A great story teller."

"Highly recommended not only as a traveller's tale but also a guide to wild camping."

"A great book to have in your bag."

The English Coast to Coast Walk – What it's really like and how to do it.

Have you ever wondered what it would feel like to walk across an entire country?

How about one as rich in history, landscape and tradition as England?

To start at one sea and to finish at another.

John Davison shows you how to walk 192 miles across England on one of the most famous hikes in the world: the Coast to Coast Walk, either by having your luggage carried or by backpacking and camping.

With detailed route assessments and all the information you need to keep yourself fed and watered on the trail, it's more straightforward than you might think!

Danby Wiske is the lowest point on the walk, physically because it stands only 35m above sea level and psychologically because its only pub never seems to open. With all the promise of a mirage showing an oasis in the desert, it looks to be a fully functioning pub but it wasn't open when I lunched on the green there and it wasn't open when Julia Bradbury passed through, making her BBC TV documentary on the CTC. It wasn't open for Wainwright either, so see if you can do better.

Connect with the Author

Check my website for help planning your own trip, at

www.johndavison.moonfruit.com

If you have any questions, email me via the "Contact" button and I'll do my best to answer them.

Keep up-to-date with my latest adventure by following me on Twitter: @bootsonthehill.

Happy trekking!

24201542R00095

Printed in Great Britain
by Amazon